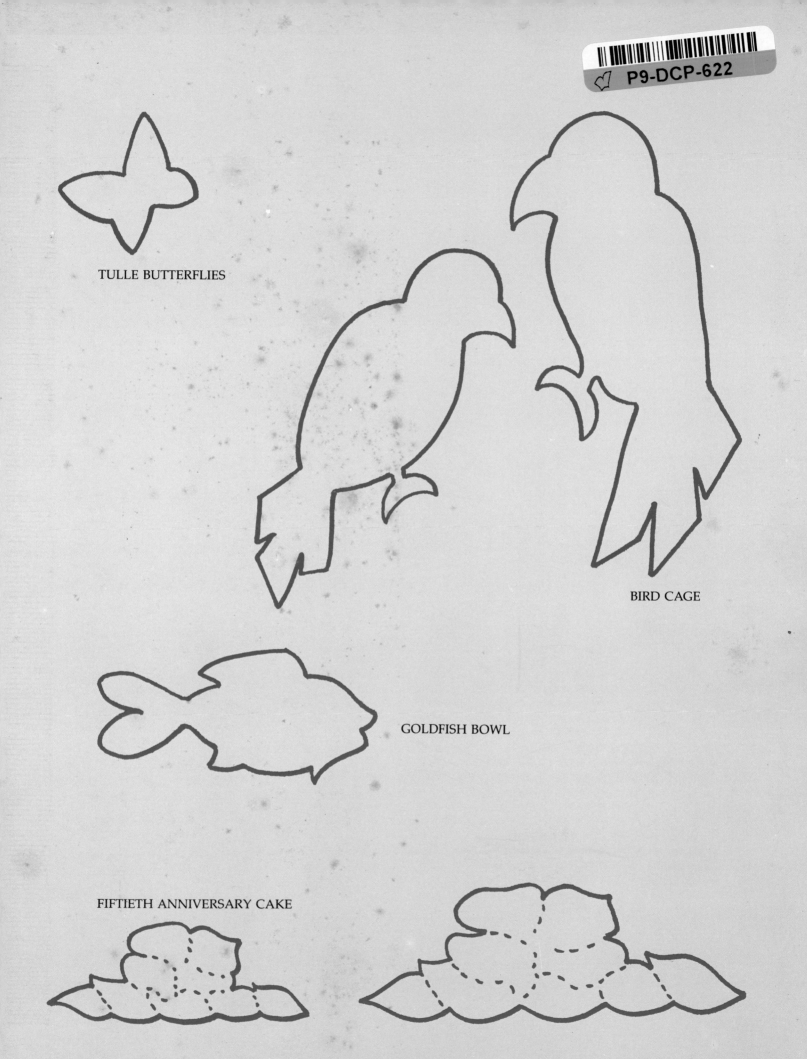

TULLE BUTTERFLIES

BIRD CAGE

GOLDFISH BOWL

FIFTIETH ANNIVERSARY CAKE

Creative CAKE
DECORATING

CAKE *Creative* DECORATING

JOANNA FARROW

MAGNA BOOKS

A QUINTET BOOK
This edition published in 1992 by
Magna Books
Magna Road, Wigston
Leicester, LE8 2XH

ISBN 1-85348-431-8

This book was designed and produced for
Quintet Publishing Limited
6 Blundell Street
London N7 9BH

Art Director: Peter Bridgewater
Editor: Josephine Bacon
Photographer: Paul Forrester

Typeset In Great Britain by
Central Southern Typesetters, Eastbourne
Manufactured in Hong Kong by Regent
Publishing Services Limited
Printed in Hong Kong by Leefung-Asco Printers
Limited

Contents

• SPECIAL EQUIPMENT •

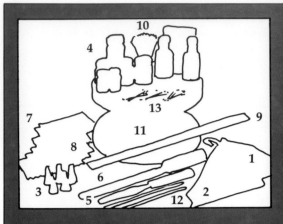

Unless you are going to make numerous cakes there is little point in spending money on expensive equipment. Here are some general items you may find useful, some of which you probably already have.

1 *Nylon piping bag* – available in a range of sizes. Ideal for piping large quantities. Easy to wash. Wears well.

2 *Disposable piping bags* – quick and cheap to make (see page 16) and ideal for piping small quantities. Also available in packs from cake decorating specialists.

3 *Icing nozzles* – many types are available but generally writer nozzles (no. 0, 1, 2 and 3) small, medium and large stars, and basket nozzles are most useful.

4 *Food colourings* – available in several forms. Liquid colours are ideal for painting but do not always produce strong tints when mixed or moulded (molded) into icing (frosting). Paste colours tend to be stronger, produce richer tones and are also ideal for painting. Gold and silver colourings are painted on but sometimes are not edible. Check with the supplier. Gold and silver lustre (in tubes) produce a delicate sparkle on icing and are edible.

5 *Small palette knife (metal spatula)* – for spreading icings (frostings), particularly around sides of cakes.

6 *Large palette knife (metal spatula)* – for spreading icings (frostings), particularly on top of cakes.

7 *Plain plastic scrapers* – for smoothing icing (frosting) around sides of cakes.

8 *Fancy plastic scrapers* – for smoothing icing (frosting) around sides of cakes where a decorative finish is required.

9 *Icing frosting ruler* – for smoothing Royal Icing over top of cake.

10 *Wooden cocktail sticks* – for easing 'poured' icing into corners and for precision work where fingers are too clumsy.

11 *Turntable* – enables you to rotate cake. Not essential, but worth it if you do lots of cake decorating.

12 *Paintbrush* – for painting colour onto cakes and dusting off cornflour (cornstarch).

13 *Flower stamens* – form the centres of open roses and other flowers.

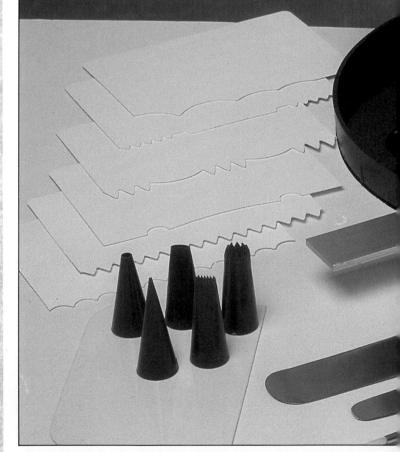

PREPARING CAKE TINS (PANS)

All tins (pans) must be greased and lined before filling with cake mixture. Use nonstick baking paper and melted margarine, shortening or oil. Brush the base and sides of the tin (pan) first.

To line a round or square tin (pan) *cut a strip of paper about 1cm/½in wider than depth of tin (pan) and long enough to line all sides (with larger cakes, you will need to cut more than 1 strip).*
Make a 1cm/½in fold along one long side. Make cuts from the edge of the paper to the folded line. Arrange the strip around the sides of tin (pan) so the folded line tucks neatly into the lower edges of the tin (pan) and the cut edges overlap around the base. (For a square tin (pan) make sure the lining is pressed well into the corners.)

Cut a round or square of paper the size of tin (pan) *base and press it into position. Lightly grease the paper. Use same technique for 900g/2lb loaf tin (pan). To line 1.1L/2pt pudding basin (small bowl) brush the base and sides with melted fat. Cut out a circle of nonstick baking paper 15cm/6in in diameter. Make 4cm/1½in cuts around the edges. Press the paper into the base so the cut edges overlap and come a little way up the sides. Lightly grease the paper.*

To prepare empty cans for novelty-shaped cakes *remove top and base of can with an opener. Peel off the paper wrapper. Wash and dry the can and stand it on a baking tray. To line the cans, use same technique as for a round cake tin (pan).*

To line a 28cm/11in by 19cm/7½in shallow cake tin (pan) *Cut out a rectangle of nonstick baking paper measuring 35.5cm/14in by 28cm/11in. Press it into the greased tin (pan). Make cuts at the corners and press the paper into the corners of the tin (pan) so the excess overlaps it. Lightly grease the paper.*

• QUICK CAKE MIX •

This 'all-in-one' cake recipe is almost as moist as a Victoria Sandwich but firmer, so more suitable for cutting into novelty cake shapes. It is ideal for children, who often dislike rich fruit cake, and can be made even more appealing if you add their favourite flavouring. Choose one of the variations below or experiment with your own.

Cakes made from Quick Cake Mix can be kept for up to 3 days in the refrigerator and up to 2 months if frozen, provided they are not iced (frosted). Thaw frozen cakes in the refrigerator and do not ice (frost) stored cakes until the day before they are to be eaten.

BASIC RECIPE
1 cup/225g/8oz soft margarine
1 cup/225g/8oz caster sugar
5 eggs
1¼ cups/275g/10oz self-raising flour
2.5ml/½ tsp baking powder
15ml/1 tbsp milk

● Set oven at 170°C/325°F/Gas 3. Grease a tin (cake pan) and line it with greased nonstick baking paper (see chosen recipe). Place all ingredients in a bowl and beat well with an electric whisk or wooden spoon for 1 to 2 minutes until evenly blended. (Don't beat mixture any more than necessary.) Turn into the prepared tin (pan) and bake for the time stated in recipe, until it is well risen and the surface feels just firm to the touch. Leave in the tin (pan) for 5 minutes then turn out onto a wire rack. Peel off the nonstick baking paper and leave cake to cool completely. Wrap in foil until ready to ice (frost).

Variations

Chocolate Substitute 4 tbsp/50g/2oz cocoa powder for 4 tbsp/50g/2oz of the flour.

Orange or Lemon Add the grated rind of 1 orange or lemon. Substitute 15ml/1 tbsp juice for the milk.

Coffee and Walnut Dissolve 30–45ml/2–3 tbsp instant coffee powder or granules in 15ml/1 tbsp boiling water. Use in place of the milk. Stir in ¼ cup/50g/2oz chopped walnuts.

Cherry and Coconut Add ¼ cup/50g/2oz chopped glacé (candied) cherries and substitute 2 tbsp/ 50g/ 2oz desiccated (shredded, unsweetened) coconut for 2 tbsp/25g/1oz of the flour.

Spicy Fruit Add 2 tbsp/50g/2oz mixed dried fruit and 10ml/2 tsp ground mixed spice.

Pastel Stir in 5ml/1 tsp blue, red or green food colouring, depending on the child's favourite.

• RICH FRUIT CAKE MIX •

A deliciously moist and spicy rich fruit cake suits all occasions – whether it's for Christmas, a Wedding, Anniversary, Engagement, Christening or, of course, a special Birthday.

The flavour of the cake improves if left to mature for a few months, so if possible make in good time. Store in a cool, dry place still wrapped in the non-stick baking paper in which it was baked and covered tightly in a double thickness of foil. During storage the flavour can be further improved by the addition of brandy. Unwrap the cake and pierce the surface with a skewer. Brush with brandy and re-wrap. (The amount added is up to you and can be one or several tablespoons.)

● Set the oven at 140°C/275°F/Gas 1. Grease the tin (pan) and line it with nonstick baking paper (see chosen recipe). For ingredients see the chart below.

Sift together the flour, salt and spice and reserve. Cream butter or margarine with the sugar until light and fluffy. Beat in the eggs, one at a time, with a little of the sifted flour to prevent curdling. Fold in the sifted flour mixture. Cut the cherries into quarters and add them to bowl with mixed peel, almonds, lemon rind, sultanas (golden raisins), currants and raisins. Stir well until evenly combined. Turn the mixture into the prepared tin and smooth the surface, making a slight dip in centre of cake; this will produce a flatter cooked cake.

Bake in the oven for time stated in chart overleaf (or chosen recipe if cooking an unusual shape).

To test if the cake is done, insert a skewer into centre. It should come out moist but without mixture sticking to it.

Leave the cake to cool completely in the tin (pan). When cold, remove it, wrap it and store it in an airtight metal container.

• INGREDIENTS CHART FOR RICH FRUIT CAKE •

Round Tin	15cm/6in	18cm/7in	20cm/8in	23cm/9in	25cm/10in	28cm/11in
Square Tin	—	15cm/6in	18cm/7in	20cm/8in	23cm/9in	25cm/10in
Ingredients						
Plain (all-purpose) flour	1¼ cups/ 150g/ 5oz	1½ cups/ 175g/ 6oz	2 cups/ 225g/ 8oz	3 cups/ 350g/ 12oz	4 cups/ 450g/ 1lb	5 cups/ 575g/ 1lb 4oz
Salt	pinch	pinch	1.25ml/ ¼ tsp	2.5ml/ ½ tsp	2.5ml/ ½ tsp	3.75ml/ ¾ tsp
Mixed spice (apple or pumpkin pie spice)	5ml/ 1 tsp	5ml/ 1 tsp	7.5ml/ 1½ tsp	10ml/ 2 tsp	15ml/ 1 tbsp	20ml/ 4 tsp
Butter or margarine	½ cup/ 125g/ 4oz	⅔ cup/ 150g/ 5oz	¾ cup/ 190g/ 6½oz	1 cup/ 250g/ 9oz	1⅔ cup/ 375g/ 13oz	2 cups/ 425g/ 15oz
Soft dark brown sugar	¾ cup/ 125g/ 4oz	1 cup/ 150g/ 5oz	1½ cup/ 190g/ 6½oz	1¾ cup/ 250g/ 9oz	2½ cup/ 375g/ 13oz	3 cups/ 425g/ 15oz
Eggs	2	3	3	4	6	8
Glacé (candied) cherries	¼ cup/ 50g/ 2oz	¼ cup/ 50g/ 2oz	½ cup 65g/ 2½oz	½ cup 75g/ 3oz	¾ cup 150g/ 5oz	1 cup 175g/ 6oz
Chopped mixed peel	1 tbsp/ 25g/ 1oz	1 tbsp/ 25g/ 1oz	1½ tbsp/ 40g/ 1½oz	2 tbsp/ 50g/ 2oz	3 tbsp/ 75g/ 3oz	½ cup/ 125g/ 4oz
Chopped almonds	3 tbsp/ 25g/ 1oz	3 tbsp/ 25g/ 1oz	5 tbsp/ 40g/ 1½oz	6 tbsp/ 50g/ 2oz	½ cup/ 75g/ 3oz	1 cup/ 125g/ 4oz
Grated lemon rind	2.5ml/ ½ tsp	2.5ml/ ½ tsp	375g/ ¾ tsp	5ml/ 1 tsp	7.5ml/ 1½ tsp	10ml 2 tsp
Sultanas (golden raisins)	¾ cup/ 125g/ 4oz	1 cup/ 175g/ 6oz	1½ cups/ 225g/ 8oz	2 cups/ 300g/ 11oz	2½ cups/ 425g/ 15oz	3 cups/ 550g/ 1lb 3oz
Currants	1 cup/ 150g/ 5oz	1¼ cups/ 200g/ 7oz	1½ cups/ 250g/ 9oz	2 cups/ 375g/ 13oz	2½ cups/ 450g/ 1lb	3 cups/ 575g/ 1lb 4oz
Raisins, seedless	¾ cup/ 125g/ 4oz	1¼ cups/ 175g/ 6oz	1½ cups/ 225g/ 8oz	2 cups/ 300g/ 11oz	2½ cups/ 425g/ 15oz	3 cups/ 550g/ 1lb 3oz
Baking time at 140°C/275°F/Gas 1	1½–2 hrs	2 hours	3–3½ hrs	3½–4 hrs	4–4½ hrs	5 hours

• ALMOND PASTE •

Apart from its 'taste appeal' almond paste has several purposes as an undercoat for traditionally iced cakes. It is used to patch up any 'gaps' in rich fruit cake, to prevent the cake discolouring the icing, and to provide a smooth surface to work on. It can also be used as a cake covering without icing (frosting), ideal for those who find other cake coverings too sweet.

This recipe produces a paler result than the traditional store-bought almond paste. However, a good quality store-bought marzipan is a good substitute if time is short or you only need a small quantity.

Almond paste can be applied as soon as the cake has cooled but leave the paste for about a week to dry out before covering it with icing (frosting).

BASIC RECIPE

2 cups/225g/8oz blanched, ground almonds (almond meal)

½ cup/125g/4oz caster (fine) sugar

1 cup/125g/4oz icing (confectioner's) sugar, sifted

1 egg

2.5ml/½ tsp almond or vanilla essence (extract)

● Place the almonds and caster (fine) sugar in a bowl. Add the icing (confectioner's) sugar and mix well. Beat the egg with the almond or vanilla essence (extract) and add to bowl. Mix to a stiff paste with your hands. Mix the ingredients no more than necessary, as overworking it may cause the oil in the almonds to discolour the icing. Wrap in foil or polythene (plastic) and store in a cool place until required.

• APRICOT GLAZE •

● Sieve 45ml/3 tbsp apricot jam into a small saucepan. Add 10ml/2 tsp water and heat through gently until jam has dissolved. Brush onto the cake while still warm.

TO COVER A CAKE WITH APRICOT GLAZE & ALMOND PASTE

1 *On a surface sprinkled with icing (confectioner's) sugar, roll out half the almond paste into a round or square slightly larger than the top of cake. Place the paste on greaseproof (wax or parchment) paper. Brush the top of cake with apricot glaze (see recipe above) and invert it on to the almond paste.*

2 *Using a palette knife (spatula), press the paste firmly into cake, filling the gap around the edges of the cake. Trim off the excess paste. Turn the cake right side up and peel off the paper. Place the cake on a board.*

3 *For a round cake, measure the circumference of the cake with a piece of string. Brush the sides of cake with apricot glaze. Roll out half the paste into a strip wide enough to cover the depth of the cake, and half the length of measured circumference. Lay it around the side of the cake. Roll out the remaining paste and use it to cover the remaining half of the side.*

4 *For a square cake, brush the sides of the cake with apricot glaze. Roll out the paste and cut out 4 rectangles, each wide enough to cover the depth of the cake, and the length of one side. Secure each to the cake.*

• WEDDING CAKE QUANTITY •
ALMOND PASTE

BASIC RECIPE

12 cups/1.25kg/3lb blanched, ground almonds (almond meal)

3 cups/750g/1½lb sugar

6 cups/750g/1½lb icing (confectioner's) sugar

6 eggs/3 tsp almond or vanilla essence (extract)

• ROYAL ICING •

Royal Icing is probably the most difficult icing (frosting) to make and use – but with a little practice both flat icing (frosting) and piping can quickly be mastered.

The consistency varies depending on the purpose. For flat coverings and piping scrolls and stars, the icing (frosting) needs to be stiff and should not stick to your finger if gently touched. For piping with writer nozzles, it needs to be slightly thinner and for pouring it needs to be thinned with egg white or water until quite runny. A batch can be thinned with egg white or water and thickened with extra icing (confectioner's) sugar as required.

Once made, Royal Icing quickly develops a crust so always keep it covered with a damp cloth and store it in the refrigerator when not in use, where it will keep for up to 2 days.

For flat, iced cakes, apply three thin layers leaving at least 24 hours between each coat.

BASIC RECIPE

2 egg whites

450g/1lb icing (confectioner's) sugar, sifted

● Place egg whites in a bowl and beat lightly with a wooden spoon. Gradually add the icing (confectioner's) sugar, beating well after each addition, until icing (frosting) is smooth and stands in soft peaks.

Note *The quantities of Royal Icing used on the cakes vary according to individual recipes but the technique for making it remains the same.*

HOW TO FLAT ICE A CAKE

1 *Spread royal icing over top of cake, working back and forth with a palette knife (spatula) to eliminate air bubbles from the icing (frosting).*

2 *Scrape an icing (frosting) ruler held at a 45° angle towards you across the top of the cake in a continuous, fluid motion. Repeat until the surface is smooth.*

3 *For a square cake, spread icing (frosting) along one side of cake with palette knife (spatula). Holding a plastic scraper at the far corner (at an angle of about 45°), draw the comb along the icing (frosting) towards you until smooth. Trim the excess along top edge and at the corners with a knife. Repeat on the opposite side. Ice the remaining sides in the same way, if possible leaving two coated sides to harden first.*

4 *Icing (frosting) a round cake is best done on a turntable, or use an upturned bowl, so you can turn the cake with one hand while icing (frosting) with the other. Scrape the sides while turning in one continuous movement.*

5 *Icing the cake board adds a more professional finish. Spread a thin layer of icing over board once sides have completely dried. Smooth around sides with the tip of a palette knife (spatula). Clean sides of board with a damp cloth.*

• MOULDING ICING (MOLDING • FROSTING)

This is great fun to use as it can be moulded (molded) to any shape (rather like plasticine) making all sorts of novelty cakes well within the cakemaker's grasp! And if you are not happy with the shape you've moulded (molded), simply re-knead and start again.

Moulding icing (molding frosting) also makes a softer (and far quicker) alternative to Royal Icing as a cake covering and is ideal for those who prefer a softer texture – although it will eventually set hard too.

Once made, wrap icing (frosting) tightly in foil or polythene (plastic) and keep for up to 24 hours. Cornflour (cornstarch), rather than icing (confectioner's) sugar, is used when rolling and shaping, as it helps produce a smoother surface and excess can easily be dusted off with a paint brush once the icing (frosting) has hardened. If you only need a very small quantity, you can buy ready made icing (frosting) in conveniently-sized packages.

The liquid glucose or corn syrup are added to the mixture to prevent crystallization and keep the icing (frosting) pliable.

BASIC RECIPE
2 egg whites
60ml/4 tbsp liquid glucose or 2 tbsp light corn syrup
900g/2lb icing (confectioner's) sugar, sifted
food colourings, optional
cornflour (cornstarch) for dusting

● Place the egg whites and liquid glucose or corn syrup in a bowl. Gradually add the sifted icing (confectioner's) sugar, working them with a wooden spoon until the mixture is too stiff to stir. Knead it into a firm ball. (You may find it easier to turn the mixture out onto a work surface and knead in the sugar as it becomes stiff.) Dot the icing (frosting) with food colouring, if using, and knead in on a surface dusted with cornflour (cornstarch).

If you find that the icing (frosting) is too soft when you roll it – losing its shape and becoming sticky – knead in more icing (confectioner's) sugar. If it's too dry and has a tendency to crack, brush with water and re-knead.

HOW TO COVER A CAKE WITH MOULDING ICING (MOLDING FROSTING)

1 *Dust a work surface with cornflour (cornstarch). Roll out the icing (frosting) into a round or square 10cm/4in larger than top of cake. Using hands dusted with cornflour (cornstarch), carefully slide your hands under the icing (frosting) and drape it over cake.*

2 *Using hands lightly dusted with cornflour (cornstarch), smooth the icing (frosting) over the top and down the sides of the cake. (Pay particular attention to corners and edges, as icing (frosting) may crack if overstretched). Mould (mold) the icing (frosting) to fit around the base of the cake and trim off the surplus with a knife. Using hands dusted with plenty of cornflour (cornstarch) 'polish' surface of cake until very smooth.*

3 *Covering the surface of the cake board gives a professional finish. Dampen the board with water. Roll out the trimmings and cut out thin strips. Fit them around the edge of the board. If the cake is square, cover one side at a time and mitre the icing (frosting) at the corners to fit.*

• BUTTERCREAM •

Buttercream is the easiest type of icing (frosting) for quick cakes. It is particularly suited to young children's birthday cakes. Buttercream can be brightly coloured, piped, and used on novelty cakes, although it cannot be moulded (molded).

  Use buttercream on sponge (yellow or pound) cakes (as both filling and covering) but not on rich fruit cakes. Once 'sealed' in buttercream, cakes will keep moist for up to 2 weeks if kept in a cool place. Any unused buttercream will freeze well for another time.

BASIC RECIPE
150g/5oz butter or margarine, softened
225g/8oz icing (confectioner's) sugar, sifted
15ml/1 tbsp boiling water

● Place butter or margarine in a bowl with the icing (confectioner's) sugar and beat well with an electric whisk or wooden spoon until combined. Add water and beat until smooth and creamy.

Variations

Chocolate Substitute 25g/1oz/2 tbsp sifted cocoa powder for 25g/1oz/2 tbsp of the icing (confectioner's) sugar.

Coffee Dissolve 30ml/2 tbsp coffee powder or granules in 15ml/1 tbsp boiling water. Use in place of water in the recipe.

Orange or Lemon Substitute grated rind and juice of 1 orange or lemon for boiling water.

Honey Omit water and substitute 30ml/2 tbsp clear honey for 25g/1oz/1 tbsp of the icing (confectioner's) sugar.

• QUICK AMERICAN FROSTING •

Almost meringue-like in texture, this soft white icing (frosting) makes a quick covering for sponge cakes. Once made, it must be used immediately to avoid a crust forming. Any variations may be added before whisking.

BASIC RECIPE
2 egg whites
350g/12oz sugar
pinch of cream of tartar
45ml/3 tbsp hot water

● Place all ingredients in a bowl over a saucepan of hot water (just removed from the heat). Whisk until mixture stands in soft peaks. This takes about 7 minutes with an electric whisk and 10 to 12 minutes with a balloon whisk. Use immediately.

Variations

Peppermint Add 5ml/1 tsp peppermint essence (extract).

Brown Sugar Substitute soft light brown sugar for the sugar.

Pastel Add 5ml/1 tsp red, pink, yellow, green or blue food colouring.

Orange or Lemon Add grated rind and 5ml/1 tsp juice of orange or lemon.

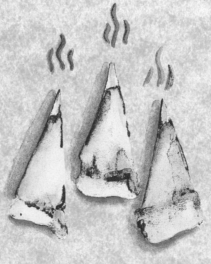

MOULDING (MOLDING) FLOWERS & LEAVES

To make moulded roses *Make up a batch of Moulding Icing (Molding Frosting) (page 13). Colour it appropriately. Place a small piece of icing (frosting) on a surface, shaping it to a point at the top.*
Take another piece and form it into a petal shape. Wrap the petal shape around the base so that the top of the petal is level with the top of the base.
Make more petals and press around the rose, overlapping petals and making them larger as you build it up.
Bend back outer petals with finger and thumb.
Slice off the base with a knife and leave to harden on baking parchment or foil.

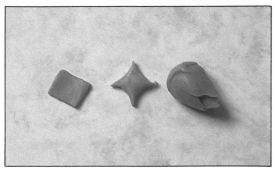

To make rosebuds *Mould (mold) the icing (frosting) into shape in the same way, but only make 2 or 3 petals, so the flower still looks closed.*
To make the bases of the rosebuds, cut out small squares of green icing (frosting) and shape each corner to a point between your fingers. Dampen one side and secure it to the base of the bud.

To make carnations *Colour the moulding icing (molding frosting) if necessary. Roll out the icing (frosting) into a strip about 18cm/7in long and 2.5cm/1in wide. Using a cocktail stick dusted with cornflour (cornstarch), press indentations all along one side of strip.*
Roll up the strip along plain edge.
Open out the flower and trim off any excess around the base.
Transfer it to nonstick baking paper, wax paper or foil to harden.

To make cut-out flowers *Colour the Moulding Icing (Molding Icing) if necessary and roll out thinly on a surface dusted with cornflour (cornstarch).*
Using 2.5cm/1in and 1cm/½in plain cutters cut out rounds.
Make 4 small indentations around the edges of the flowers with a knife.
Pierce a hole in centre with a skewer. Slightly 'cup' the flowers and leave them on nonstick baking paper, wax paper or foil to harden.

To make leaves *Colour Moulding Icing (Molding Frosting) green and roll out thinly on a surface dusted with cornflour (cornstarch). Cut out small leaf shapes with a thin bladed knife.*
Vary the sizes of the leaves so they look more realistic.
Mark the veins with a knife.
Transfer to the nonstick baking paper, wax paper or foil to harden.

• SECURING MOULDED (MOLDED) • SHAPES

By pressing a cocktail stick into shaped pieces of icing (frosting) and leaving it to harden, all sorts of attachments can be added to novelty cakes to make them more fun. Discard them before slicing the cake.

Mould (mold) the appropriate shape out of Moulding Icing (Molding Frosting) (see page 13) and press a cocktail stick into the end which will eventually lie against the cake. Transfer it to a sheet of nonstick baking paper, wax paper or foil and leave it to dry. This takes about 2 days with home-made Moulding Icing (Molding Frosting), but it can take longer if you use the bought variety.

Peel away the paper or foil and press the shape into the cake. If liked, make a hole first with another cocktail stick so the shape slips into place very easily. With delicate shapes it's worth making a 'spare' in case of breakage.

ROYAL ICING RUN-OUTS

Run-outs are raised shapes of Royal Icing used for decorative borders and names. The outline is first piped, then filled in with very thin Royal Icing.

Note *For filling in small areas and writing with icing (frosting) it is easier to place thinned icing (frosting) in a paper piping bag and cut off tip for piping. This way you have better control.*

Mark the outline of the shape required. Place the appropriately coloured icing (frosting) in a piping bag fitted with a writer nozzle (no. 1) and pipe a continuous line over outlined shape. Leave to dry.

Thin down more icing (frosting) with unbeaten egg white or water to a cream-like consistency, so that when spoon is lifted from bowl, the icing (frosting) loses its shape in seconds.

Carefully spoon the icing (frosting) into the centre of the outline. Push it into the edges and corners with a cocktail stick, and prick any air bubbles. Leave to set.

BASKET WORK

This is much easier to do than you would imagine. If you are a beginner, it is wise to practise first on paper or card.

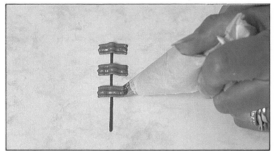

1 *Using an icing bag fitted with a writer nozzle (no. 2), pipe a vertical line. Using another icing bag fitted with a basket nozzle, pipe 2.5cm/1in bands across the vertical line, leaving the width of the nozzle space between each band.*

2 *Pipe another vertical line down the edge of the basket bands. Pipe more basket lines across the second line, filling in gaps left by first bands.*

CHOCOLATE RUN-OUTS

Chocolate can easily be re-shaped by melting and leaving to harden. It tends to be rather fragile once run-out, so use cool hands when transferring it to the cake. Should it break while being secured to the cake, simply re-melt it and start again.

1 *Break the chocolate into small pieces and place in a bowl. Stand the bowl over (not in) a pan of water which has just been removed from the heat. Leave until melted. Alternatively, chocolate can be melted in a microwave oven on the lowest setting.*

2 *Pour the melted chocolate onto a piece of nonstick baking paper or wax paper on a board. Tilt the paper so the chocolate coats the surface evenly.*

3 *Cut out the required shape with a sharp, thin-bladed knife. Carefully peel away the paper and secure the run-out to the cake.*

● TULLE BUTTERFLIES ●

Tulle is a delicate netting available from haber-dashery (dry goods) and fabric shops and usually comes in an assortment of colours. If you have difficulty finding it, rice paper makes a good substitute.

Make a template (see endpapers) for the butterfly. Use it to cut out the tulle shapes. Fold the tulle through the centre of butterfly so it looks as if it is in flight.

Place some Royal Icing (page 12) in a piping bag fitted with a writer nozzle (no. 1) and pipe along the underside of the fold. Secure the butterfly to the cake and leave it to set. Using the same nozzle, pipe around the edges of the butterflies.

● USEFUL TIPS ●

● To ensure that larger-sized rich fruit cakes do not overcook around the edges, before baking wrap several thicknesses of brown paper or newspaper around cake, securing them with string. Check the oven after half the cooking time; if the surface of the cake begins to overbrown, cover it loosely with a double thickness of greaseproof or nonstick baking paper. Do *not* use foil which will prevent steam escaping and produce a doughy result.

● Don't throw away trimmed pieces of sponge cake when cutting novelty shapes. Freeze them for making trifle or other desserts at a later date.

● Pipe buttercream left in the piping bag into rosettes and freeze them on greaseproof or wax paper for use on another cake. Transfer them to the cake while still frozen.

● If tightly wrapped in cling film (plastic wrap) all icings (frostings) will keep for several days in refrigerator.

● If adding colour to a whole batch of moulding (molding) icing (frosting) knead it in while icing is still fairly moist. By the time you have achieved the right texture, your icing (frosting) will also be evenly coloured.

● Butter used straight from the refrigerator can be softened in a mixing bowl in the microwave oven.
● Do not discard the egg yolks when using the whites to make icing (frosting). Place them in a freezer bag with a pinch of salt and refrigerate until required.

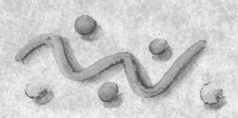

To make a greaseproof piping bag:
Cut a 25cm/10in square from greaseproof (wax or nonstick baking) paper and fold in half diagonally.

Hold the paper at the centre of the folded side and twist one extreme point round to meet central point forming a cone shape. Fold other point over in the same way.

Fold over corners at edges to retain shape. Cut off about 1cm/1½in at point and drop in icing nozzle. Fill with icing (frosting) and fold over bag at open end.

To make a 'disposable' serrated icing scraper

If it's just for one cake, this decorative scraper can be improvised using firm card and a pair of pinking shears. Cut the card to an 11.5cm/ 4½in by 8cm/3½in rectangle. Cut one long side with pinking shears.

● An ordinary ruler can make an adequate substitute for an icing ruler if you don't have time to visit or order from a cake decorating specialist. Choose one that does not bend easily and without deep indentations along marked side.

● The flavourless caramel used for gravy browning or colouring microwave foods makes a good substitute for beige or brown colouring.

● You needn't stock a whole larder of different food colourings. Don't forget that the three primary colours, blue, red and yellow can make a whole rainbow of colours themselves:
mix equal drops of blue and yellow for green
mix two drops blue and one red for violet
mix two drops yellow and one red for orange
mix three drops yellow and one red for peach

● When adding colour to moulding icing (molding frosting) or Royal Icing bear in mind that colours darken on drying.

● Where necessary, colours that are too bright can be toned down with brown or black colouring e.g., a little brown food colouring added to green makes moulded (molded) leaves look far more realistic.

● If you want to colour Plaster of Paris cake pillars pastel or cream to match the cake, dip them quickly in water coloured with a few drops of appropriate colour. Test the strength of the colour first on base of one pillar.

The
Cakes

Cakes for Kids

There's nothing more rewarding than watching a child's face light up as you present them with a special cake – candles glowing – on that all-important birthday. And if you can make it in a novelty shape that depicts their favourite toy or latest craze, then so much the better. Fortunately for busy parents, children's cakes tend to be easy too. A brightly-covered Quick Cake Mix (page 9) is always as well received as any complicated masterpiece. The following recipes from the very simple to the slightly more involved, are all fun to make and may inspire you to try out your own creation for the next big event!

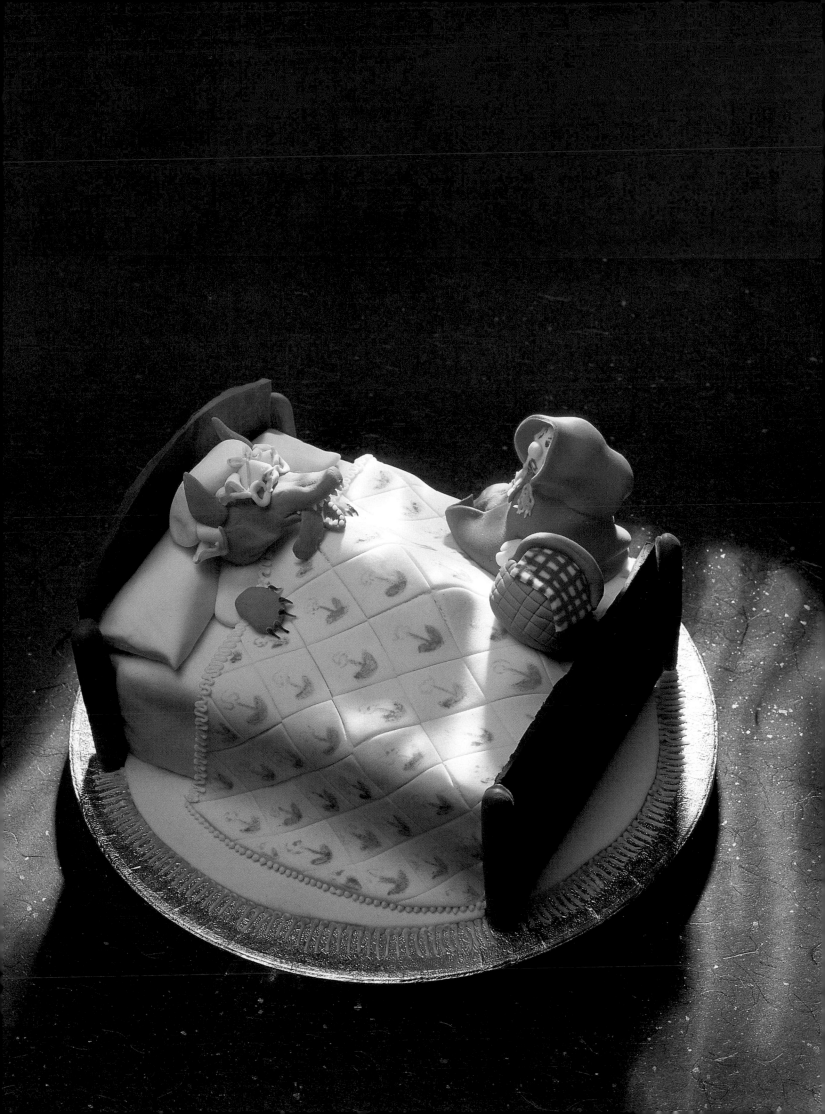

Red Riding Hood

Don't be put off by the intricate looking detail – all you need is a little patience!

INGREDIENTS

15cm/6in square Rich Fruit Cake (pages 9 and 10)
1 quantity Apricot Glaze (page 11)
1 quantity Moulding Icing (Molding Frosting) (page 13)
cornflour (cornstarch) for dusting
25cm/10in round silver cake board
125g/4oz plain (semisweet) chocolate
green, red, cream, brown and blue food colourings
10 chocolate finger biscuits (cookies)
45ml/3 tbsp icing (confectioner's) sugar

● Cut a 2.5cm/1in slice from one side of the cake. Secure the slice with Apricot Glaze to one short side to make a rectangle. Trim off the surplus. This is the bed.

● Colour a little moulding icing (molding frosting) beige and roll it out on a surface dusted with cornflour (cornstarch) into a 20cm/8in round. Lay it on the board to make the rug. Position the cake on the board. Brush the cake with more Apricot Glaze.

● To make the headboard and footboard of the bed, melt the chocolate and spread it thinly on a sheet of nonstick baking paper or wax paper. Leave to set. (See Chocolate Runouts, page 17.) Cut out a 12.5cm/5in by 6.5cm/2½in rectangle. Cut out all but one long side of a second rectangle measuring 12.5cm/5in by 7.5cm/3in. Cut the remaining side in a curve to shape the headboard of the bed. Cool your hands under cold water and position chocolate run-outs at short ends of cake. Secure a chocolate finger biscuit at each corner with remaining Apricot Glaze, to make the bedposts.

● Roll out a wide strip of moulding icing (molding frosting) and position at top end of cake. Pile remaining chocolate fingers in centre of cake to make wolf's body. It will not be visible, just a lump under the covers.

● Roll out more icing (frosting) into a large rectangle to make the bedspread. Make diagonal markings with a knife (being careful not to cut right through icing (frosting)) and position the 'bedspread' on cake. Shape more icing into two pillows and position them on the bed.

● Divide remaining icing (frosting) into four. Colour one piece red, one cream, one brown and leave remainder white. Shape a small piece of cream icing into a thin sausage and position between pillow and bedspread to make the wolf's shoulders. Form another piece into a ball for Red Riding Hood's head. Secure a small nose on the face with a little water. Shape two small pieces of icing into hands and reserve. Form the remaining icing (frosting) into a round and secure it to the bed-

spread to make Red Riding Hood's body. Position her head on top. Shape a little red icing (frosting) into a tongue and reserve it. Roll out the remaining red icing (frosting) very thinly and wrap it around Red Riding Hood's body to form a cloak. Cut a slit on either side of cloak for armholes, and position her hands.

● Shape a little brown icing (frosting) into a basket. Mark lines on it with a sharp knife and secure it to the bed. Knead a little red food colouring into the remainder to make a richer colour. Shape this into the wolf's head and paws and secure it to his shoulders.

● Roll out a thin strip of white icing (frosting) and secure it to the wolf's head, gathering it up slightly to make mob cap frill. Shape more icing (frosting) into a ball. Flatten it to 0.5cm/¼in thickness and place on top of head for the cap. Roll small pieces of icing (frosting) very thinly between your fingers and shape them into glasses. Roll another piece of white icing (frosting) into a square. Use it to cover the basket.

● Place the icing (confectioner's) sugar in a bowl. Thin it down with a little water to the consistency of thick cream and place in a piping bag fitted with a writer nozzle (no. 1).

● Use it to pipe wolf's teeth, claws, trim on hat, Red Riding Hood's hair and edging on bedspread and carpet. Leave overnight to harden.

● To finish, paint the carpet edging, flowers on bedspread, Red Riding Hood's hair, basket napkin, wolf's claws, glasses and cap in the appropriate colours.

(see picture on page 21)

Goldfish Bowl

Try to form a good bowl shape by neatly trimming and filling the gaps in the sandwiched cake before starting to ice. Don't go to the expense of buying a second mixing bowl if you only have one; bake half at a time.

INGREDIENTS

1 quantity Quick Cake Mix (page 9)
1 quantity Apricot Glaze (page 11)
1 quantity Moulding Icing (Molding Frosting) (page 13)
cornflour (cornstarch) for dusting
20cm/8in round silver cake board
blue, orange, brown, green and red food colourings
60ml/4tbsp demerara (light brown) sugar

● Grease and line bases of two 2½pt/1.1L ovenproof glass mixing bowls. Divide Quick Cake Mix between bowls and level surfaces. Bake for about 40 to 50 minutes or until the surfaces feel firm to the touch.
● Slice the tops of the cakes level and discard the slices. Sandwich the cakes together with apricot glaze. Fill in gaps around the join with the moulding icing (molding frosting). Roll out a little icing (frosting) very thinly on a surface dusted with cornflour (cornstarch) and use to cover board. Mark the icing (frosting) into 1cm/½in squares with the back of a knife. Reserve a quarter of the icing (frosting) and colour the remainder blue. Roll out and drape it over cake. Smooth the icing (frosting) down the sides of the cake, trimming the lower edge to fit. Roll out the trimmings into a long thin sausage. Dampen the underside with water and position it around top of bowl for rim. Paint an uneven band of water around base of bowl and press the sugar against it to make the gravel.
● Colour a little icing (frosting) orange and shape the goldfish, using the template given. Use trimmings to shape a goldfish head for the top of the cake. Secure the fish to the cake with a little water.
● Shape three bubbles in white icing (frosting) and the small signpost in brown icing (frosting). Secure to cake. Place remaining icing (frosting) in a mixing bowl. Thin it down with water to piping consistency and colour it green. Place the icing (frosting) in a piping bag fitted with a number 2 nozzle and pipe plants. Paint the birthday message, 'NO FISHING' sign and gingham on cloth.

'Squeeze Me' Bear

This cake makes a rather appealing 'toy' too, as the central button on teddy's sweatshirt is a small squeak cushion. A joke shop is the most likely place to see them.

INGREDIENTS

1 quantity chocolate flavoured Quick Cake Mix (page 9)
double quantity chocolate flavoured Buttercream (page 14)
covered board, measuring about 40cm/16in by 30cm/12in
½ quantity Moulding Icing (Molding Frosting) (page 13)
cornflour (cornstarch) for dusting
cream, red and brown or black food colourings
2 brown chocolate buttons

● Divide Quick Cake Mix among 4 18cm/7in sandwich tins (shallow round cake pans). Bake for 25 to 30 minutes. When completely cool, cut two of the cakes following diagram.

● Sandwich the two uncut cakes with a little buttercream on board. (This forms teddy's body.)

Sandwich the remaining pieces and secure to the body in the appropriate places. Scoop out a circle in the centre of the cake to allow for the 'SQUEEZE ME' button. Use the remaining buttercream to cover the cake completely, fluffing it up with a fork.

● Shape 2 small buttons, about 2.5cm/1in diameter, and a 'T' from moulding icing (molding frosting). Reserve. Colour a quarter of the icing (frosting) cream colour and remainder red. Roll out red icing (frosting) on a surface dusted with cornflour (cornstarch). Lay over teddy's body and shape for sweatshirt pressing into the cavity in the centre of cake. Reserve trimmings. Use cream-coloured icing (frosting) to shape paws, feet and snout. Secure to cake. Position chocolate buttons for eyes.

● Shape the red icing (frosting) trimming for the mouth and nose. Secure the mouth, nose, buttons and 'T' with a little water. Press the squeak button into the cavity in the sweatshirt and write 'SQUEEZE ME' in brown or black food colouring.

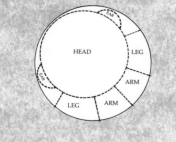

Happy Face Clock

Any child learning to tell the time will love this birthday clock with hands that actually move. Set the hands at the number denoting the child's age.

INGREDIENTS

1 quantity Quick Cake Mix (page 9)
1 quantity Buttercream (page 14)
green, yellow, red, brown and blue food colourings
1 cup/225g/8oz white Almond Paste (page 10)
20cm/8in round silver cake board
red candles
a little card
1 cocktail stick

● Bake Quick Cake Mix in a 20cm/8in round cake tin for about 1 hour, until surface feels firm.

● Colour the buttercream green and spread it around the sides and outer edge of the top of cake. Draw a fork from the base of the cake over the top edge to make a decorative pattern. Repeat all around cake. Colour half the Almond Paste yellow and roll it out in a 16.5cm/6½in round. Press on to the top of the cake. Use a wide metal spatula to turn the cake on one side and position on cake board. Colour remaining Almond Paste red. Shape a small piece into a round, about the size of a cherry, and reserve for nose. Shape another piece into a larger round, flatten slightly and place on top of cake to support candles. Press candles into the paste.

● Divide the remaining almond paste into four and roll into balls. Position for clock feet. Using brown food colouring to paint clock numbers, eyes and eyebrows. Paint a large red mouth and colour eyes blue.

● Using the template (see endpapers) cut out clock hands in card. Make a hole in each end with a pin and press the cocktail stick through holes and into centre of clock face leaving 1cm/½cm of stick exposed. Press the reserved nose on to the cocktail stick to secure.

Chattanooga Choo-Choo

If you're feeling really ambitious, this cake could be further enhanced with a Buttercream stream and grassy bank under the bridge.

INGREDIENTS

1 quantity Quick Cake Mix (page 9)
1 quantity chocolate flavoured Buttercream (page 14)
30cm/12in round silver cake board
½ quantity Almond Paste (page 10)
red food colouring
½ quantity Apricot Glaze (page 11)
450g/1lb liquorice allsorts or round candies (for making train wheels, chimney, etc.)
candles and holders

● Bake the Quick Cake Mix in a 25cm/10in square cake tin (pan) for about 1 hour or until the surface feels firm to the touch. When completely cooled, cut the cake following the diagram.

● Sandwich the two long strips of cake together with Buttercream and place this sandwich on the board. Cut out a small 'archway' from the lower cake. Cover the cake with Buttercream and make brickwork markings with a sharp knife.

● To make the train, colour the almond paste red and roll it out thinly. Use to cover the sides of the two small pieces of cake for the trucks (boxcars), securing them with Apricot Glaze. Cut out a 12.5cm/5in by 5cm/2in rectangle and reserve it for the base of the engine. Cover the cylindrical cake with Almond Paste and secure a slightly domed piece of paste at one end for the front of the train. Cover the remaining piece of cake with paste for the driver's (engineer's) cab, shaping the sides and roof as shown.

● Slice a liquorice allsort or round candy into three for the wheels. Chop plain liquorice for coal and halve square liquorice or candies to decorate the bridge walls. Position the rectangular engine base on bridge, lifting it off surface slightly with spare sweets (candies). Secure the driver's cab and engine with Apricot Glaze and position the trucks (boxcars) behind the engine.

● Press candles and holders into the trucks and surround them with chopped liquorice. Complete the cake with liquorice decorations.

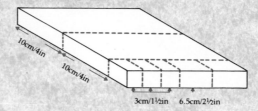

Building Blocks

This cake is specially designed for a toddler's birthday party. At the end of the day, each partygoer can take home a 'complete' cake in the shape of a building brick.

INGREDIENTS

1 quantity Quick Cake Mix (page 9)
1 quantity Moulding Icing (Molding Frosting) (page 13)
pink, blue and violet food colourings
1 quantity Apricot Glaze (page 11)
cornflour (cornstarch) for dusting
20cm/8in square silver cake board
candles

● Bake Quick Cake Mix in an 18cm/7in square cake tin for about 1 hour until the surface feels firm to the touch. When completely cooled cut the cake into nine squares, trimming the top of cake level so squares are even sided.

● Divide Moulding Icing (Molding Frosting) into four. Colour one piece pink, one blue and one violet, leaving the remainder white. Brush the sides of the cakes with apricot glaze.

● Roll out the icing (frosting), one colour at a time, on a surface dusted with cornflour (cornstarch). Cut squares to cover each side (except the base) of the cakes, pinching the edges together to form neat cubes.

● Stack the cakes attractively on the board and leave the icing (frosting) to harden slightly. Using a fine paintbrush and blue food colouring, paint the child's name and age on the blocks. Decorate any remaining blocks with simple shapes, and position candles on holders to finish.

Space Shuttle

A llow several days for the wings to dry before positioning them on the cake. The horizontal candles may be inclined to drip so be prepared!

INGREDIENTS

1 quantity Moulding Icing (Molding Frosting) (page 13)

cornflour (cornstarch) for dusting

18cm/7in square quantity Rich Fruit Cake mixture (page 9)

38cm/15in by 25cm/10in board, covered with shiny blue paper

1 quantity Apricot Glaze (page 11)

cocktail sticks

black, red and blue food colourings

60ml/4 tbsp icing (confectioner's) sugar

3 red candles and holders

● Roll out a little moulding icing (molding frosting) on a surface dusted with cornflour (cornstarch) to 0.5cm/¼in thickness. Cut out two wings each, measuring 19cm/7½in at the longest side, and 9cm/3½in at the shortest side. Curve the third side to shape the outer edge of the wings. Shape a third triangle for a tail. Press 2 cocktail sticks into one side of the tail for securing to cake once hardened

(see page 16). Leave the cake on nonstick baking paper, wax paper or foil for at least 2 days, for the wings to dry.

● Divide the Rich Fruit Cake mixture between three 400-g/14oz lined empty cans (see page 8). Bake for about 1 hour 30 minutes or until a skewer inserted into the centre comes out clean. Shape the cakes following the diagram. Place on the board sandwiching together with apricot glaze. Brush the sides with the remaining glaze.

● Roll out the remaining icing (frosting) and use to cover all the sides of the cake. Using a knife mark a line all around cake 2.5cm/1in up from base. (The area beneath this line will be painted black.) Mark the window in the same way.

● Press 4 cocktail sticks, horizontally into each side of cake along marked line. (These will support the wings), Leave the cake to dry.

● Using appropriate food colourings paint the space shuttle, writing the name and age of the child along the sides. Mix the icing (confectioner's) sugar with a little water to make a thin paste. Use to secure the wings and tail to the cake. Press the candles and holders into the end of the cake.

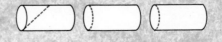

Rainbow's End

A simple design that's well within the grasp of last minute cakemakers. Use bought almond paste to save time.

INGREDIENTS

1 quantity Quick Cake Mix (page 9)
1 quantity Buttercream (page 14)
25cm/10in square silver cake board
red, yellow, green and blue food colourings
½ cup/125g/4oz Almond Paste
candles and holders

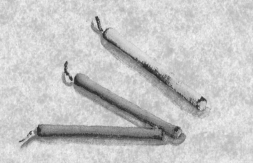

● Bake the Quick Cake Mix in a 20cm/8in round cake tin for about 1 hour or until the surface feels firm to the touch. When completely cooled, slice the cake into two semi-circles. Cut out a small semi-circle from the base of each cake to form rainbow arcs. Sandwich the cakes side-by-side with a little Buttercream, and arrange them on the board.

● Divide the Buttercream between four bowls, varying the quantities in each bowl, as only a small amount of red is needed, compared to the blue. Colour each portion red, yellow, green and blue.

● Spread the red Buttercream under the arc of the rainbow and add a band around the front. Spread a second band of yellow Buttercream, above the red one. Continue with the green and then the blue Buttercream, spreading blue Buttercream on the top of the cake. Run the tines of a fork along the bands to make a decorative pattern.

● Colour half of the Almond Paste yellow. Reserve a little paste for the umbrella and shape the remainder into a sun. Position the sun at one end of rainbow. Shape the remaining almond paste into cloud, umbrella and raindrops and paint in the appropriate colours. Position the sun at the other end of the rainbow. Press the candles and holders into the top of the cake.

Bird Cage

Equally well-suited to house zoo animals, this fun cake will appeal to animal lovers of any age – although they'll never know where to start cutting it!

INGREDIENTS

20cm/8in square quantity Rich Fruit Cake mixture (page 9)
double quantity Almond Paste (page 10)
1 quantity Apricot Glaze (page 11)
20cm/8in round silver cake board
red, blue, green and yellow food colourings
about 30 lengths of uncooked spaghetti
2 2.5cm/1in lengths chocolate flake

● Spread a thin layer of Rich Fruit Cake mixture in each of 2 15cm/6in sandwich tins (shallow round cake pans). Divide the remaining mixture between two 780g/1lb 14oz lined empty cans (see page 8). Bake the mixture in the cans for about 2 hours, and the mixture in tins for about 1 hour or until a skewer inserted in centre comes out clean.

● To make the parrots, roll out a little Almond Paste to 0.5cm/ ¼in thickness and cut out two parrots using the template (see endpapers). Paint them in bright colours using red, blue, green and yellow food colourings. Reserve.

● Level the surfaces of the cakes baked in the cans by trimming off the excess. Brush all the cakes with Apricot Glaze. Roll out the Almond Paste and use it to cover tops of the large, shallow cakes. Place one shallow cake on the board. Sandwich the cylindrical cakes together one on top of the other and cover the sides with Almond Paste. Position them in the centre of the cake on the board. Top with the remaining cake. Brush the backs of parrots with Apricot Glaze and secure them to the cylindrical cakes. Press the chocolate flake bars into the cake under the parrots to make perches.

● Trim the spaghetti lengths to exact height of cage and press them around the sides of cake, spacing them about 2cm/¾in apart. Roll out Almond Paste trimmings into strips, 2cm/¾in wide and the length of the circumference of the cake. Wrap one strip around the base of the cake to conceal the uncovered cake edges and the ends of spaghetti. (You may find it easier to roll it out and secure it in shorter lengths.) Using a 2.5cm/1in plain pastry (cookie) cutter mark an attractive border around the paste strips. Use Almond Paste trimmings to shape a small handle and secure it to the top of the cake.

Snowman

A mint-flavoured frosting would suit this wintry birthday cake. As only a little Almond Paste is needed, it might be easier to use store-bought marzipan.

INGREDIENTS

1 quantity Quick Cake Mix (page 9)
125g/4oz icing (confectioner's) sugar
50g/2oz desiccated (shredded) coconut
green, orange, brown and red food colourings
25cm/10in round silver cake board
candles and holders
1 quantity Quick American Frosting (page 14)
½ cup/125g/4oz Almond Paste (page 12)
raisins

● Use a little of the Quick Cake Mix to half fill a 20cm/8in sandwich tin (shallow round cake pan). Divide the remaining mixture between two 780g/1lb 14oz lined empty cans (see page 8). Bake the mixture in the tin (pan) for 25–30 minutes and the mixture in the cans for 45 to 55 minutes or until surfaces feel firm to the touch.

● Beat the icing (confectioner's) sugar in a bowl with about 15ml/1 tbsp water to make a thin paste. Place the coconut in a separate bowl and beat in a little green food colouring. Spread two thirds of the paste icing (frosting) over the board and sprinkle it with the coloured coconut to make the grass. Make holes for the candle holders with a skewer or knitting needle and press the holders into the board about 1cm/½in from the edge.

● Place the cake baked in sandwich tin (shallow round cake pan) in the centre of the board. Trim the top of one remaining cake level and centre it on the first cake. Place the untrimmed cake on top, securing the cakes in place with the remaining icing (frosting) paste.

● Use the Quick American Frosting to cover the entire cake, spreading it on to the grass around the candle holders. Leave the icing to set firmly overnight.

● Colour a little Almond Paste orange, and shape it into a carrot. Position it on the face as a nose. Use the raisins for the buttons and mouth. Roll out a little Almond Paste and cut out strips, about 1cm/½in wide. Use for the scarf, and paint it brightly.

● Colour remaining Almond Paste brown and position two small pieces to make eyes. Shape the remainder into a hat. Position all these items on the cake. Insert the candles into the holders.

Cakes for Teenagers

This is by far the most difficult age group to please, even when it comes to cakes. Candles are out (unless specifically requested) and at the risk of being 'old-hat' more than a little imagination is required regarding theme. Sport, music, and very up-to-the-minute games might provide inspiration, but if you get really stuck there's one subject that won't fail to please – fast 'food', such as an Ice Cream Soda or Deep Pan Pizza.

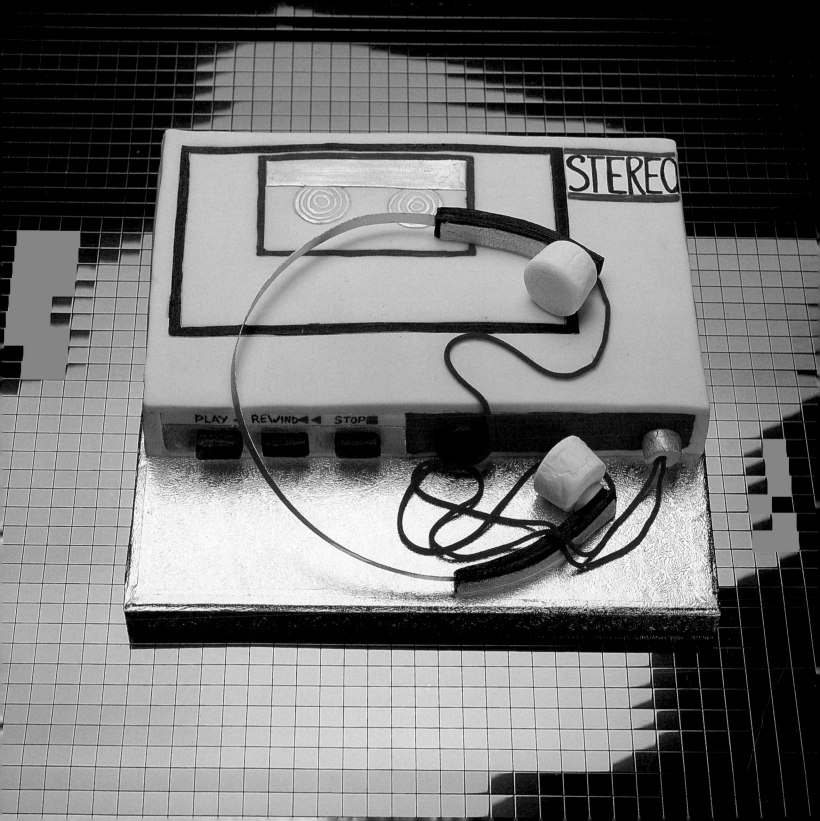

Stereo Cassette Player

This is a very easy cake to decorate, but looks so effective. You can use the Quick Cake Mix (page 9), baked in the same tin (pan), for an even quicker version.

INGREDIENTS

1 square quantity Rich Fruit Cake for 18cm/7in square tin (pan) (page 9)
28cm/11in square silver cake board
1 quantity Apricot Glaze (page 11)
¾ quantity Moulding Icing (Molding Frosting) (page 13)
cornflour (cornstarch) for dusting
thin strip of card 35.5cm/14in long and 0.5cm/ ¼in wide, painted with silver colouring
red, black and silver food colourings
2 red or black liquorice 'bootlaces'
2 white marshmallows

● Bake the Rich Fruit Cake mixture in a 28cm/11in by 19cm/ 7½in rectangular shallow cake tin (pan) for about 2 hours 30 minutes or until a skewer inserted into the centre comes out clean. When completely cooled trim the sides of the cake to form a straight-sided rectangle. Place it on a board and brush it with apricot glaze.

● Roll out the moulding icing (molding frosting) on a surface dusted with cornflour (cornstarch). Cut it to fit the sides of the cake, brushing with water and sealing where the corners meet. Roll out the remaining icing (frosting) and use it to cover the top of the cake, reserving the trimmings.

● Using a thin-bladed knife, make shallow cuts in the icing (frosting) to mark the controls and cassette areas. Shape 3 small rectangles of icing and position them on the control panel. Shape a round piece of icing for the volume control and plug socket. Roll out the trimmings and cut out 4 strips, each measuring 7.5cm/3in by 1cm/½in. These are the holders for the marshmallow 'earphones'. Sandwich each end of the card between 2 strips, securing with water.

● Position the card on the cake bending it to make headphones. Secure a marshmallow to each end of headphones with a little icing (frosting). Position the liquorice 'bootlaces', pressing ends into headphones and plug socket. Use red, black and silver food colourings to paint appropriate parts of cake.

(see picture on page 33)

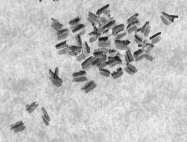

Sports Bag

If you enjoy moulding fiddly shapes, here's the cake for you. The wide liquorice 'handles' look particularly effective, but if you can't get hold of any, roll strips of icing (frosting) and paint them.

INGREDIENTS

20cm/8in round quantity Rich Fruit Cake mixture (page 9)
1 quantity Moulding Icing (Molding Frosting) (page 13)
brown, violet, silver, red and blue food colourings
cornflour (cornstarch) for dusting
20cm/8in square silver cake board
1 breadstick, about 15cm/6in long
1 quantity Apricot Glaze (page 11)
60ml/4tbsp icing (confectioner's) sugar
several wide strips of liquorice (totalling about 81cm/32in in length)

● Divide Rich Fruit Cake mixture between two 780g/1lb 14oz lined empty cans (see Preparing Cake Tins (Pans), page 8). Bake for 2 hours or until done. Trim the surfaces of cakes level.

● To cover the board with 'wood effect' flooring, dot a quarter of the Moulding Icing (Molding Frosting) with a little brown food colouring. Roll it out to a long thin rope on a surface dusted with cornflour (cornstarch) and fold in half. Keep rolling and folding until the icing (frosting) is streaked with colouring. Roll out the icing (frosting) thinly and use it to cover the board, securing it with water.

● Knead the trimmings together and wrap them around the breadstick. Wrap a piece of white icing (frosting) around one end of the stick. Press the white icing (frosting) over a fine cheese grater to create a towelling effect. Leave the racket to harden.

● Brush the cake with Apricot Glaze. Colour three-quarters of the icing (frosting) violet. Use it to cover all sides of the cake. Arrange the cake on the board with the icing join facing upwards. Pull the join apart slightly to represent the opening in the bag. Roll out two thin strips of icing (frosting), about 18cm/ 7in long and 0.5cm/¼in wide. Make small cuts in the strips and secure the strips to the edges of the bag opening to represent the zipper. Paint it silver. Mix the icing (confectioner's) sugar with a little water to make a thin paste, and use this to secure the liquorice to the bag for handles.

● Use the remaining icing (frosting) to shape items in the bag. Wedge the breadstick in the top to serve as the racket handle. Roughen towelling surface with a cheese grater and paint items in appropriate colours. Pipe laces on to shoes.

Sports Bag

Deep Pan Pizza

Silver food colouring is inedible so discard the 'pan' before eating. For an edible alternative use silver lustre (available from cake decorating specialists) or colour the icing (frosting) brown or grey.

INGREDIENTS

1 quantity Rich Fruit Cake for 15cm/6in round cake (page 9)
25cm/10in round silver cake board, covered with shiny black paper
1 quantity Apricot Glaze (page 11)
1 quantity Moulding Icing (Molding Frosting) (page 13)
brown, red, yellow, green and silver food colourings
cornflour (cornstarch) for dusting
2 cocktail sticks

● Bake Rich Fruit Cake mixture in an 18cm/7in round cake tin (pan) for about 2 hours 30 minutes or until a skewer inserted into centre comes out clean. When completely cooled, trim the sides of cake with a sharp knife to give it a pan shape. Place the cake on a board and brush the top and sides with Apricot Glaze.

● Colour a quarter of the Moulding Icing (Molding Frosting) pale brown and use it to cover top of cake. Smooth the surface with hands dusted with cornflour (cornstarch). Roll out two-thirds of remaining icing (frosting) into strip 5cm/2in wide and long enough to wrap around the sides of the cake. (You may find it easier to do this in two separate pieces.) Place the strip in position. Colour half the remaining icing (frosting) red. Reserve a small piece for the centre of the olives. Divide the remainder in half. Break off small pieces from one half and scatter them over the top of the cake to resemble tomatoes or peppers. Thin down the second half to a thick paste with water, and brush it over the top of the cake leaving a little of the brown base exposed around the edges. Colour a little more icing (frosting) yellow and grate it over cake, using a metal cheese grater.

● Colour more icing (frosting) brown, roll it out and shape into 'anchovy fillets'. Position them on the cake. Roll reserved red icing (frosting) into a thin sausage. Colour a little icing (frosting) green and wrap it around the red icing (frosting). Cut it widthways into slices and position it on the cake to resemble olives.

● To make handles for the pan: roll out some white icing (frosting) to two thin pencil-shapes about 9cm/3½in long. Form them into handles. Halve cocktail sticks and press a half into each end of the handles. (See Securing Moulded (Molded) Shapes to Cake, page 16.) Transfer to foil and leave to set overnight.

● Gently press the exposed ends of the cocktail sticks into the icing (frosting) around the sides of the cake so the handles sit on the edges of the pan. Paint the pan silver and lightly paint edges of the 'bread base' a darker shade of brown.

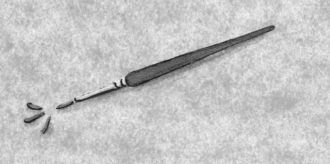

Computer Game

This novelty design can be made equally well using Moulding Icing (Molding Frosting) (page 13). If you are feeling artistic, paint the current favourite game on the screen.

INGREDIENTS

1 quantity Quick Cake Mix (page 9)
25cm/10in square silver cake board
1 quantity Apricot Glaze (page 11)
double quantity Almond Paste (page 10)
yellow, blue, black and red food colourings
mint or spearmint sweets (candies)
1 cocktail stick

● Half fill a 900g/2lb loaf tin (pan) with Quick Cake Mix. Spoon the remainder into a 20cm/8in square cake tin (pan). Bake the mixture in the cake tin (pan) for 35 to 40 minutes and mixture in loaf tin (pan) for 50 minutes to 1 hour.

● Place the square cake on the board and brush it with Apricot Glaze. Cover the top, then each side of cake with Almond Paste. Brush the second cake with Apricot Glaze and cover it with Almond Paste, trimming off the excess at the base and corners. Brush one side of loaf cake with Apricot Glaze and position on square cake. Roll out more Almond Paste and cut out a rectangular computer screen. Round off the corners and secure it to cake with Apricot Glaze. Using a knife, mark a line around sides of loaf cake, 1cm/½in away from front edge.

● Paint behind the marked line and around the side of the square cake with yellow food colouring. Paint the computer screen pale blue, paint remaining almond paste black, leaving a panel unpainted for the controls. Position the sweets (candies) on the cake, securing them with a little glaze. Cut the remaining controls out of Almond Paste and position on cake, securing the joystick to the cake with cocktail stick. Paint the controls and symbols on the screen in the appropriate colours. Use black colouring to write a message on screen and keys.

Car Cake

A driving test pass is always worthy of a celebration cake. The model used could be the new driver's own car, or the car he or she dreams of owning. Add suitable license plates such as 'UR 16', and this could become a birthday cake.

INGREDIENTS

1 quantity Quick Cake Mix (page 9)
a few chocolate biscuits or chocolate chip cookies
board measuring 40cm/16in by 20cm/8in
1 quantity Apricot Glaze (page 11)
1 quantity Moulding Icing (Molding Frosting) (page 13)
cornflour (cornstarch) for dusting
blue, black, red and silver food colourings
2 square clear boiled sweets (candies)
125g/4oz sugar
a little beaten egg white

● Spoon a 1cm/½in depth of Quick Cake Mix into a 900g/2lb loaf tin (pan). Turn remainder into a 28cm/11in by 19cm/7½in rectangular shallow cake tin (pan). Bake the mixture in loaf tin (pan) for about 30 minutes and the mixture in cake tin (pan) for about 50 minutes or until surfaces feel firm to the touch.
● Place a row of the biscuits (cookies) on the board and cover them with the large cake. (This raises the car body up off the board.) Brush the cake with the Apricot Glaze. Trim the top of the smaller cake level and slope the sides of the cake to form the top of the car. Position the car on the base. Cut out small wheel arches in appropriate parts of cake base.
● Reserve a quarter of the moulding icing (molding frosting). Colour the remainder blue. Roll out the icing (frosting) into a 30-cm/12-in by 25-cm/10-in rectangle and lay it over the cake. Dust your hands with cornflour (cornstarch) and use them to smooth the cake.
● Press the icing (frosting) under the cake and into the wheel arches, trimming it to fit where necessary.
● Using a sharp knife, make lines over icing (frosting) to indicate the boot (trunk), bonnet (hood), doors and radiator. Press the boiled sweets (candies) into the icing (frosting) for headlights.
● Roll out a little white icing (frosting) to 0.5cm/¼in thickness. Cut out four circles, 3cm/1¼in in diameter and fit them into the wheel cavities, securing with a little water. Roll and cut out two long strips of icing (frosting) 1cm/⅓in wide and 25cm/10in long. Secure one strip to front of car and one to back for bumpers. Shape two more pieces for licence plates and secure to bumpers.
● Shape two small squares of icing for 'L' plates, if used. Colour a little icing cream colour and shape into an arm. Secure the 'L' plates to the arm. Press a cocktail stick into the arm and leave to thoroughly

dry on nonstick baking or wax paper. (See Securing Moulding Icing (Molding Frosting) Shapes to Cake, page 16.) (It's worth making two arms in case one breaks!) Shape 2 small 'matchsticks' of icing and reserve for the windscreen wipers.
● Colour the remaining icing (frosting) grey (using black food colouring). Roll it out and shape for windows. Secure them to the cake. Shape a small triangle of icing and position it for an emblem on the bonnet (hood).
● Beat a little black food colouring into the sugar to make it gravel colour. Brush the exposed board with egg white and sprinkle with the sugar. Leave the cake to dry overnight.
● Paint the outer edges of wheels black. Paint the appropriate parts of the car with silver food colouring. Paint red 'L's' on the plates and a message on the licence plate. Secure the windscreen wipers to the windshield. Press the arm on to a cocktail stick and into the window to finish.

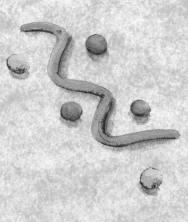

Car Cake

Ice Cream Soda

Small round sweets (candies) form the bubbles on this cake, or you could use small balls of coloured Moulding Icing (Molding Frosting) instead.

INGREDIENTS

20cm/8in round quantity Rich Fruit Cake mixture (page 9)
1 quantity Moulding Icing (Molding Frosting) (page 13)
cornflour (cornstarch) for dusting
3 cocktail sticks
pink, green and yellow food colourings
1 quantity Apricot Glaze (page 11)
15cm/6in round silver cake board
90ml/6 tbsp icing (confectioner's) sugar
about 125g/4oz small round sweets (candies)
a few clear mint sweets (candies)

● Divide Rich Fruit Cake mixture between 2 780g/ 1lb 14oz lined empty cans (see page 8). Bake for about 2 hours. Level the surface of one cake.
● Using an ice cream scoop or tablespoon, scoop out 2 balls of Moulding Icing (Molding Frosting) to form ice cream. (With a little practice you should be

able to make the scooped edges look just like real ice cream.) To make the straws, dust the work surface with cornflour (cornstarch) and roll out more moulding icing (molding frosting) to 2 thin rolls, about 10cm/4in long. Trim the ends. Make several bands of cuts into the straws, about 5cm/2in from one end, to form the bendy parts of the straws. Bend the straws slightly, and press a cocktail stick into other ends for securing them to cake, once hardened. Shape a swizzle stick out of a little pink coloured icing (frosting).
● Press a cocktail stick into the end in the same way. Transfer the shaped moulding icing (molding frosting) to nonstick baking paper, wax paper or foil and leave to harden.
● Sandwich the cakes together with Glaze to form the tall glass. (The trimmed cake should go underneath.) Brush the surfaces with remaining glaze.
● Colour the remaining icing (frosting) pale green and use it to cover the sides of the cakes. Place them on the board. Blend the icing (confectioner's) sugar with a little water to make a thin paste. Press the straws and swizzle stick into the cake and secure the ice cream with a little paste. Secure bubbles and mints to the cakes with more paste. Paint straws, a band of colour around the cake and a message on the swizzle stick, if liked.

Making a Wish

This might just suit the request for an elegant cake 'with a difference'. It would also make an unusual design for an 18th birthday cake with the '18' painted on the girls's collar or on the mini cake in the picture.

INGREDIENTS

20cm/8in Rich Fruit Cake (page 9)
1 quantity Apricot Glaze (page 11)
double quantity Almond Paste (page 10) (optional)
25cm/10in square silver cake board
1 quantity Moulding Icing (Molding Frosting) (page 13)
cornflour (cornstarch) for dusting
1 quantity Royal Icing (page 12)
red and black food colourings
91cm/3ft red ribbon, about 3cm/1¼in wide

● Brush the cake with apricot glaze and cover it with almond paste, if liked. Place it on the board and cover it with the moulding icing (molding frosting), smoothing down the sides of the cake with hands dusted with cornflour (cornstarch). Use the trimmings to cover the edges of the board.

● Following the instructions under Tracing Off Templates (see endpapers), transfer the template of the face design on to the cake.

● Place a little royal icing in a piping bag fitted with a writer nozzle (no. 3). Use it to pipe the outline of the collar, the lower outline of the hat and the piping on the cake in picture. Place more icing (frosting) in a piping bag fitted with a writer nozzle (no. 1) and pipe the remaining outlines. Use more royal icing in a bag fitted with a medium sized star nozzle to pipe a scroll around the top and lower edges of cake.

● Use the remaining icing (frosting) to make run-outs for the hat, hair, ear-ring, mouth and collar areas (see Royal Icing Run-outs, page 16). Leave to set.

● Paint cake in appropriate colours and secure ribbon with a little icing (frosting).

Cakes for Adults

Fun cakes needn't be another childhood treat that you leave behind. If you're stuck for a present, a cake baked in a favourite hobby shape might be just the answer. Rich fruit cake is usually popular but you may prefer to substitute a recipe that you know is well liked, provided it will fit, or trim to fit, the appropriate tin size. If you want to add candles, press them into the cake board – first making holes with a skewer so the holders slide in with ease.

Get Knitting

Knitting no longer has an 'old lady in a rocking chair' image and so this easy cake should appeal to everyone. If you prefer, use Moulding Icing (Molding Frosting) to cover the cake.

INGREDIENTS
double quantity Almond Paste (page 10)
cornflour (cornstarch) or icing (confectioner's) sugar, for dusting
20cm/8in round Rich Fruit Cake (page 9)
1 quantity Apricot Glaze (page 11)
25cm/10in round silver cake board
double quantity Royal Icing (page 12)
yellow, brown, peach and gold food colourings

● To make the needles: roll out a little almond paste on a surface dusted with cornflour (cornstarch) or icing (confectioner's) sugar until it is 18cm/7in long and about 0.5cm/¼in in diameter. Pinch each end to a point and secure 2 small flattened rounds to other ends.

● Shape 3 small pieces of almond paste, each about the size of a plum, into balls, and flatten them slightly. Transfer them to nonstick baking paper, wax paper or foil with the needles and reserve.

● Brush the cake with Apricot Glaze and cover it with the remaining Almond Paste. Place it on the board.

● Spoon about 60ml/4tbsp Royal Icing into a bowl and colour it pale yellow. Colour a second quantity pale brown and a third peach. Cover and reserve.

● Colour the remaining icing (frosting) cream (using just a dash of brown colouring) and use to flat ice cake and board.

● Position the needles on the cake as in the photograph and paint them gold. Position the three balls behind the needles. Place the yellow icing in a piping bag fitted with a writer nozzle (no. 2).

● Pipe lines to completely cover one ball. Use the remainder to pipe 3 to 4 fluted lines around top edge of cake.

● Place the brown icing in the piping bag and use it to cover the second ball. Add more fluted lines around cake. Place the peach icing in the bag and use it to cover the third ball and the last section around the side of the cake. Use the remaining icing (frosting) in the bag to outline 'HAPPY BIRTHDAY' below the needles. Fill in the outlines with wavy lines and pipe stitches at the point where wording joins needles.

(see picture on page 43)

Downhill Skier

This simple design is one which sporty friends might appreciate. Make the skier in advance, but don't position it until the last minute, in case the colours run. You can use bought Moulding Icing (Molding Frosting).

INGREDIENTS

1 quantity Quick Cake Mix (page 9)
225g/8oz Moulding Icing (Molding Frosting) (page 13)
cornflour (cornstarch) for dusting
red, blue and yellow food colourings
35.5cm/14in by 28cm/11in board, covered with shiny blue paper
1 quantity Quick American Frosting (page 13)
1 small pasta wheel
1 piece uncooked spaghetti, about 5cm/2in long
1 red lollipop
several pieces of plastic fern (available from florists)

● Bake Quick Cake Mix in a 20cm/8in square cake tin (pan) for about 1 hour or until the surface feels just firm to the touch.

● Use a little Moulding Icing (Molding Frosting) to shape the sun. Roll more Moulding Icing (Molding Frosting) into a thin roll about 10cm/4in long and bend it to form the crouched skier. Use more icing (frosting) to shape the hat, scarf, arms, boots and skis. Make 2 sets of skis, in case one breaks. Paint the sun and skier in appropriate colours and transfer them to nonstick baking paper, wax paper or foil to harden slightly.

● Cut the cake into pieces and arrange it on a board following the diagram below. Use the Quick American Frosting to cover the entire cake. Arrange the sun and skier on the cake, positioning the pasta wheels and spaghetti to make the ski sticks. Finish the cake with the lollipop post and trees made from plastic fern.

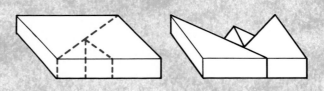

Fishing Basket

Basket work is one of the most effective piped decorations, but is really very simple to do (see page 17). The lid is made from almond paste and needs to be made several days in advance to allow it time to dry out.

INGREDIENTS

18cm/7in square quantity Rich Fruit Cake (page 9)
20cm/8in square silver cake board
1 quantity Apricot Glaze (page 11)
double quantity Almond Paste (page 10)
Royal Icing (page 12) using 3 egg whites and 6 cups/ 1½lb/750g icing (confectioner's) sugar
brown, red, blue, green, yellow and silver food colourings
few leaves of rice paper

● Bake the Rich Fruit Cake mixture in a 900g/2lb loaf tin (pan) for about 3 hours or until a skewer inserted into centre comes out clean.

● Place the cake on a board and brush it with Apricot Glaze. Roll out a little almond paste to 0.5cm/¼in thickness and cut out a 16.5-cm/6½-in by 9-cm/3½-in rectangle. Transfer the rectangle to a sheet of nonstick baking paper, wax paper or foil and leave to harden.

● Reserve 350g/12oz of the almond paste and use the remainder to thinly cover top and sides of cake. Reserve 90ml/6 tbsp Royal Icing and use the remainder to pipe basket work on lid and sides of cake following directions on page 17. Colour the reserved Royal Icing green. Place a little icing (frosting) in a piping bag fitted with a writer nozzle (no. 1 or 2) and reserve. Spread the remainder on to the board around the cake and fluff it up with a fork, to make the grass.

● Use the reserved Almond Paste to shape the contents of the fishing basket. To make a landing net, shape a thin roll of paste about 23cm/9in long. Bend it into a circle and lay it to one side of cake. Pipe criss-cross lines of reserved green icing (frosting) for netting. Pipe long grass around the basket with a little more icing (frosting).

● Shape the other items in basket using the remaining paste. (All are painted after shaping) and arrange in the basket. Arrange the items towards the front of the basket so that the lid can sit securely at an angle of 45°. Use the Royal Icing left in piping bag to secure almond paste where necessary. Paint the contents in appropriate colours and tuck the rice paper around the sandwiches and fish.

Bowl of Daffodils

Decorate this cake with the recipient's favourite icing (frosting) or almond paste.

INGREDIENTS

18cm/7in round quantity Rich Fruit Cake mixture (page 9)
double quantity Almond Paste (page 10) or 1 quantity Moulding Icing (Molding Frosting) (page 13)
1 quantity of Apricot Glaze (page 11)
20cm/8in round silver cake board
brown, green and yellow food colourings
50g/2oz raisins
6 wooden sticks, about 10cm/4in long

● Divide the cake mixture between 2 1.1L/2pt ovenproof glass bowls. Bake for about 2 hours.
● Roll out a little almond paste or icing (frosting) very thinly and use to cover board, securing with a little water. Trim the edges and mark a pattern over surface with a fluted biscuit (cookie) cutter.
● Sandwich cakes together with Apricot Glaze and fill the gaps around centre with paste or icing (frosting). Place the cake on the board and brush with the remaining glaze.

● Shape a small piece of paste or icing (frosting) about 5cm/2in by 2.5cm/1in to make the label and reserve it. Colour half the remainder brown, a small piece green and the rest yellow. Use brown paste or icing (frosting) to cover the cake. Roll the trimmings into a thin roll about 38cm/15in long and position it around the top of the cake to make a rim, securing it with water. Place raisins on top of cake to resemble soil.
● Roll out the green paste or icing (frosting) and cut out several long thin leaves. Roll out the yellow paste or icing (frosting) and, using the template given, cut out 12 daffodil shapes. Dampen the surface of half the yellow shapes with water and lay them on the end of each stick, across the cut-outs, so the ends meet in the centre. Press the remaining cut-outs over first so the ends of sticks are enclosed. Roll out the trimmings and cut out 6 rectangles measuring 6.5cm/2½in by 2cm/¾in. Flute one long side of each with a pastry wheel. Roll each rectangle into a tube and secure it to the centres of flowers with water. Leave the flowers to dry for 24 hours.
● Write a message on the label and secure it to the cake, using paste or icing (frosting) trimmings for string. Press the daffodils and leaves into the cake, first making holes in the cake with a skewer, so that the leaves are easier to press in.

Greenhouse

Greenhouse

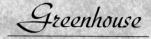

An ideal cake for a keen gardener's retirement party or special birthday, in which case rows of candles could be pressed into the 'vegetable plot'.

INGREDIENTS

18cm/7in square quantity Rich Fruit Cake mixture (page 9)
25cm/10in square silver cake board
1 quantity Apricot Glaze (page 11)
1 quantity Almond Paste (page 10), optional
1½ quantity Royal Icing (page 11)
½ quantity Moulding Icing (Molding Frosting) (page 13)
cornflour (cornstarch) for dusting
125g/4oz raisins
matchsticks
green, red, yellow, blue and brown food colourings
5ml/1 tsp black poppyseeds

● Bake the Rich Fruit Cake mixture in a 15cm/6in square cake tin (pan) for 2 hours 30 minutes or until a skewer inserted into centre comes out clean. When completely cooled, cut the cake into pieces following the diagram.

● Arrange the two 2.5cm/1in strips of cake, side by side on the board, sandwiching the join with Apricot Glaze. Position the two remaining pieces on top as shown, sandwiching with more glaze. Cover the cake with Almond Paste, if liked. (This will make the Royal Icing easier to use if you are a beginner.) Cover all sides of the greenhouse with a thin layer of Royal Icing. Roll out the Moulding Icing (Molding Frosting) to 0.5cm/¼in thickness on a surface dusted with cornflour (cornstarch). Cut out a 6.5-cm/2½-in by 4-cm/1½-in rectangle for the door, removing two panels for the windows. Transfer the rectangle to nonstick baking paper, wax paper or foil to dry out overnight.

● Cut more Moulding Icing (Molding Frosting) to make the framework over the greenhouse. (Use a little water to secure it to the sides of the cake if the Royal Icing has dried out). Roughly chop the raisins. Spread a thin layer of Royal Icing on the surface of the board to make the vegetable plot and flower bed alongside the greenhouse. Press raisins into icing (frosting) for earth.

● Press a row of matchsticks into the raisins alongside the greenhouse. Reserve 45ml/3 tbsp Royal Icing and colour the remainder green. Spread it over the rest of the board and fluff it up slightly for grass. Shape four small pieces of Moulding Icing (Molding Frosting) for the path. Sprinkle with poppyseeds and position over the grass. Use remaining Moulding Icing (Molding Frosting) to shape the cabbages and spade, using a matchstick for the handle. Place a little green Royal Icing in a piping bag fitted with a plain nozzle (no. 2 or no. 3). Use it to pipe tomato plants on to matchstick supports and the plants in the plot. Use a little reserved icing, coloured red, to pipe the tomatoes. Spread one edge of the door with the icing (frosting) and secure to front of greenhouse. Paint the plants inside the greenhouse with watered down food colourings.

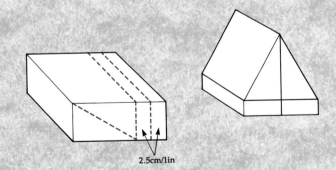

2.5cm/1in

Pineapple Gateau

A little kirsch, rum or brandy drizzled over this huge gâteau before icing (frosting) gives it an extra special flavour. The chopping board provides an ideal surface – as long as it's not one you've used for crushing garlic!

INGREDIENTS

1 quantity cherry-and-coconut-flavoured Quick Cake Mix (page 9)
board measuring about 35.5cm/14in by 28cm/11in
780-g/1lb 12-oz can pineapple rings
1 quantity Almond Paste (page 10)
green, yellow and brown food colourings
1 quantity Quick American Frosting (page 14)

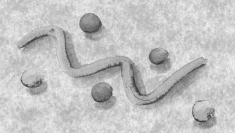

● Bake the Quick Cake Mix in a 28cm/11in by 19cm/7½in shallow cake tin for about 1 hour or until surface feels firm to the touch. When completely cold cut off corners of cake to form an oval shape. Place the cake on the board.

● Crumble the trimmed cake into a bowl. Drain the can of pineapple rings, reserving the juice. Roughly chop the fruit and mix it with the cake trimmings, adding enough of the juice to hold cake together. Mound the trimmings over the cake on the board to give pineapple shape.

● Colour the almond paste green and roll it out to 0.5cm/¼in thickness. Cut out the leaves to about 9cm/3½in long and 3cm/¼in at widest point. Place 1 leaf base downward at top of the pineapple and gradually build up the other leaves over the first, securing if necessary with water, to shape the top.

● Make the American Frosting, whisking in about 5ml/1 tsp yellow food colouring. Place it in a piping bag fitted with a large star nozzle, about 1cm/½in in diameter. Use it to pipe small blobs all over cake. (You'll probably need to fill the bag in two separate batches.) Leave the frosting to set until a crust has formed. Reserve a little frosting.

● Colour the reserved frosting brown and thin it down with water. Paint it between the blobs of frosting to highlight them.

Liqueur Chocolate Gateau

The foil-wrapped chocolate liqueur bottles make this very simple cake look attractive. If bottle-shaped, liqueur-wrapped chocolates are unavailable, use extra almond paste flavoured with liqueurs. Use more almond paste for shaping the other decorations.

INGREDIENTS

1 quantity chocolate-flavoured Quick Cake Mix (page 9)
25cm/10in round silver cake board
45ml/3tbsp rum, Cointreau or other liqueur
1 quantity chocolate-flavoured Buttercream (page 14)
1 quantity Almond Paste (page 10)
pink food colouring
cornflour (cornstarch) or icing (confectioner's) sugar for dusting
about 16 liqueur chocolates
candles and holders

● Bake Quick Cake Mix in a 20cm/8in round cake tin (pan) for about 1 hour until the surface feels firm to the touch. When completely cooled, place the cake on a board and sprinkle it with the rum, Cointreau or chosen liqueur.

● Spread the cake with Buttercream and decorate the surface, using a fluted cake scraper or a fork.

● Colour the almond paste pink and roll out on a surface dusted with cornflour (cornstarch) or icing (confectioner's) sugar. Cut out the shapes for the glasses and press them around the sides and in a circle around the top of the cake. Position a liqueur chocolate in between each. Press the candles and holders into the cake. Store the cake in a cool place until required.

Elegant Cakes

The centrepiece of any special event is always the cake –
whether it's Christmas, a wedding, coming of age
or a retirement party. Yet, however spectacular the cakes in
this section may look, they are all well within the grasp of
the amateur.
Icing (frosting) a large area does take a little practice so before
committing yourself to tackling a three-tier cake experiment
on a polystyrene mould, (mold) a strong card box set on a
cake board, or a 'practice' cake that the family will be happy
to eat even if the decoration isn't perfect!
Refer to the techniques section in the front of the book for
glazing, covering with Almond Paste and flat icing (frosting)
with Royal Icing.

Easy Wedding Cake

Wedding Cake

This simple but beautiful cake can be iced (frosted) in hours! Choose your flowers – dried ones are lovely for an Autumn wedding – and colour co-ordinate them with the icing (frosting), lace and ribbon.

INGREDIENTS

25cm/10in and 15cm/6in round Rich Fruit Cake (pages 9 and 10)
double quantity Apricot Glaze (page 11)
three-quarters Almond Paste Wedding Cake Quantity (page 12)
30cm/12in and 20cm/8in round silver cake boards
double quantity Moulding Icing (Molding Frosting (page 13)
food colouring (optional)
cornflour (cornstarch) for dusting
1.5m/5ft piece ribbon, about 0.5cm/¼in wide
1.5m/5ft gathered lace edging, about 4cm/1½in wide
fresh or dried flowers
4 cake pillars
1 small round block of green foam or similar about 6.5cm/2½in in diameter, for securing flowers (available from florists)

● Brush Rich Fruit Cakes with Apricot Glaze and cover with Almond Paste. Place on boards.
● Colour the Moulding Icing (Molding Frosting) if liked. Dust a work surface with cornflour (cornstarch), roll out the icing (frosting) and use it to cover the cakes and exposed surfaces of the boards. Leave it overnight to harden.
● Secure the lace around the base of each cake. Moisten the green foam block if using fresh flowers and stand it in a small dish so it fits snugly. Alternatively, wrap lower half of the foam in foil. Arrange the flowers and position them on cakes. Position the pillars and assemble the cake just before the reception.

(see picture on page 53)

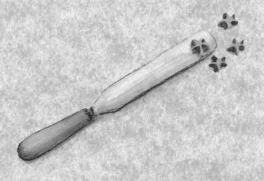

It is best to have this cake finished at least a week before the wedding, so aim to start icing (frosting) it a week in advance.

Green makes an unusual colour for decoration, but any other colour can be substituted to tie in with the general colour scheme of the wedding.

INGREDIENTS

15cm/6in square Rich Fruit Cake (pages 9 and 10)
20cm/8in square Rich Fruit Cake (pages 9 and 10)
25cm/10in square Rich Fruit Cake (pages 9 and 10)
double quantity Apricot Glaze (page 11)
Wedding Cake Quantity Almond Paste (page 12)
3 square silver cake boards, measuring 35.5cm/14in, 25cm/10in and 20cm/8in
Royal Icing for flat icing (frosting) using 14 egg whites and 28 cups/3kg/7lb icing (confectioner's) sugar
Royal Icing for decorating, using 4 egg whites and and 8 cups/900g/2lb icing (confectioner's) sugar
green and yellow food colourings
gypsophilla (babies' breath) or orange blossom
posy of flowers for top of cake
8 cake pillars

● Brush the cakes with Apricot Glaze and cover them with the almond paste. Place them on the boards and cover them with Royal Icing. Leave them to harden.
● Make a template: fold a 30cm/12in piece of non-stick baking paper in half, then fold it in half twice more, to form a triangle consisting of 8 thicknesses of paper. Make a pencil mark on one folded side 11.5cm/4½in from the tip and make another mark the same distance from the tip on the opposite side. Use a pair of compasses to draw a concave curve linking the two marks together. Cut the paper along the curve. Open out the folded paper and lay it over the largest cake. Mark the outline of the paper on the cake with a pin. Refold the paper and mark it again on each folded side, this time 9cm/3½in from the tip. Join the marks with a concave curve, as before, and cut along the curve. Open out the paper, lay it on the 20cm/8in cake and mark the outline as before with a pin. Refold the paper and cut out a third curve, marking the sides of the triangle 6.5cm/2½in from the tip. Unfold the paper and mark the outline with a pin on the smallest cake.
● Place about 30ml/2 tbsp Royal Icing for decorating in a piping bag fitted with a writer nozzle (no. 1). Use it to pipe over the marked outlines. Pipe more lines on each side of the boards, 5mm/¼in away from the edge.
● Thin more icing (frosting) with water to run-out consistency (see page 16) and use it to fill the areas between the base of the cake and the marked line. ▶

Wedding Cake

Place more icing (frosting) in a piping bag fitted with a medium star nozzle and use it to pipe a scroll border around the top and lower edges. Run-out the area between the marked outline on top of the cakes and the scroll edges. Leave to harden.

● Colour about 90ml/6 tbsp Royal Icing with green food colouring. (If the green colouring is bright, you can tone it down with a drop of black or brown food colouring.) Use the green icing (frosting) to pipe decorative borders around the sides of the cake as in the photograph.

● Colour the remaining icing (frosting) yellow, and place it in a piping bag fitted with a writer nozzle (no. 1). Use it to pipe triangles of dots around all the runout work. Use the remainder to complete the decorative borders around the sides of the cakes.

● Arrange the pillars on the cakes and decorate the cakes with the flowers. Assemble the cakes just before the reception.

American Wedding Cake

American Wedding Cake

Traditional American wedding cakes are made of sponge (yellow) cake, as opposed to rich fruit cake, and do not have pillars. American cakes are often decorated with buttercream or American Frosting, but the Moulding Icing (Molding Frosting) is easier to use.

The two top tiers in this recipe are placed on thin silver cake cards before mounting. This is not essential, but it makes cutting much easier.

AMERICAN CAKE MIXTURE

25CM/10IN ROUND:

3 cups/350g/12oz self-raising (self-rising) flour

2.5ml/½ tsp baking powder

1½ cups/350g/12oz sugar

1½ cups/350g/12oz butter or margarine, softened

6 eggs

20CM/8IN ROUND:

2 cups/225g/8oz self-raising (self-rising) flour

1.25ml/¼ tsp baking powder

1 cup/225g/8oz sugar

1 cup/225g/8oz butter or margarine, softened

4 eggs

15CM/6IN ROUND:

1 cup/125g/4oz self-raising (self-rising) flour

good pinch baking powder

½ cup/125g/4oz sugar

½ cup/125g/4oz butter or margarine, softened

2 eggs

BRANDY BUTTER:

2½ cups/575g/1¼ lb unsalted butter, softened

1 cup/175g/6oz icing (confectioner's) sugar

60ml–90ml/4 tbsp–5 tbsp brandy

TO DECORATE:

double quantity Apricot Glaze (page 11)

triple quantity Moulding Icing (Molding Frosting) (page 13)

cornflour (cornstarch) for dusting

30cm/12in round silver cake board

23cm/9in and 18cm/7in round silver cake cards

1 quantity Royal Icing (page 12)

several pieces of plastic fern or asparagus

food colouring (optional)

tulle butterflies (page 18)

small posy of flowers for top of cake

● Make one cake at a time. Grease and line the tin (pan). Set oven at 180°C/350°F/Gas 4. Place the cake ingredients in a bowl and beat well with an electric whisk or wooden spoon for 1 to 2 minutes until evenly blended. Turn them into the tin and level the surface. Bake the 25cm/10in cake for about 1 hour to 1 hour 10 minutes, the 20cm/8in cake for 50 minutes to 1 hour, and the 15cm/6in cake for 40 to 45 minutes. Transfer the cakes to a wire rack to cool.

● To make brandy butter, beat the softened butter in a bowl with the icing (confectioner's) sugar. Add the brandy and beat well until smooth.

● Split each cake horizontally and sandwich together with brandy butter. Place the largest cake on the board and brush it with apricot glaze. Dust a work surface with cornflour (cornstarch) and roll out a little Moulding Icing (Molding Frosting) on it. Use the icing (frosting) to cover the surface of the cake on the board. Roll out more icing (frosting) and use it to cover the large cake. Press the lower edge into the corners of the cake and trim the edges 2.5cm/½in away from cake.

● Place the 20cm/8in cake on the 23cm/9in cake card. Brush with Apricot Glaze and position them on the first cake.

● Cover with Moulding Icing (Molding Frosting), pressing the icing (frosting) into the lower edge, and trimming off the icing (frosting) at the edge of the card. Position and ice the smallest cake in the same way, reserving the trimmings.

● Place a little Royal Icing in a piping bag fitted with a medium star nozzle. Use it to pipe around trimmed edges of all three cakes.

● Use Moulding Icing (Molding Frosting) trimmings to make cut-out flowers (see page 15). You will need about 24 large and 15 small flowers. Secure them to the cake with the icing (frosting) in the bag. Start by positioning 3 small flowers at regular intervals around the top tier. Continue arranging the flowers, letting them trail attractively in an anti-clockwise direction as you work down the cakes.

● Colour the remaining Royal Icing if liked, and place it in a piping bag fitted with a writer nozzle (no. 1). Use it to pipe trailing lines and leaves from flowers. Make tulle butterflies following directions on page 18 using icing in bag to secure to cake and pipe outline. Secure small pieces of fern to the cake with the icing (frosting) left in the bag.

● Position the flowers on top of cake just before the reception.

Coming of Age Cake

This is a rather plain coming-of-age cake, but extra decorations and a brighter colour scheme would make it look more elaborate.

INGREDIENTS

25cm/10in Rich Fruit Cake (page 9)
1 quantity Apricot Glaze (page 11)
triple quantity Almond Paste (page 10)
30cm/12in round silver cake board
quadruple quantity Royal Icing (page 12)
black and yellow food colourings

● Bake the Rich Fruit Cake according to directions on page 10. Brush it with the Apricot Glaze and cover it with Almond Paste. Place it on the board and cover with Royal Icing.

● Using the key template and the 18 or 21 given, transfer outlines on to the cake. Using a ruler as a guide, mark diagonal lines across the cake (avoiding the surface inside the 'key') about 2.5cm/1in apart.

● Place a little icing (frosting) in a piping bag fitted with a writer nozzle (no. 1) and pipe over the outline of the key, the numbers and diagonal lines. Pipe another line around cake board 0.5cm/¼in away from outer edge. Reserve the icing in the bag.

● Place about 75ml/5 tbsp icing (frosting) in a bag fitted with a small star nozzle. Divide the remaining icing (frosting) between two bowls. Colour one portion grey (using a little black food colouring) and one yellow. Use yellow icing (frosting) to run-out the space between the base of the cake and the piping near edge of board (see page 16). Use the icing (frosting) in the bag fitted with star nozzle to pipe around top edge of cake. Use grey icing (frosting) to run-out number on key, then run-out alternating bands of yellow and grey across top of cake. Leave overnight to harden.

● Pipe a star border around the lower edge of cake. Using the icing (frosting) in piping bag fitted with writer nozzle, pipe dots all around edge of key, around the run-out on base of board and where the colours meet on the diagonal bands of coloured icing. Finish with small loops of icing (frosting) around the sides of the cake.

Christening Cake

This simple decoration works well on any size cake, round or square.

INGREDIENTS

20cm/8in square Rich Fruit Cake (page 9)
1 quantity Apricot Glaze (page 11)
double quantity Almond Paste (page 10)
30cm/12in square silver cake board
1½ quantity Moulding Icing (Molding Frosting) (page 13)
cornflour (cornstarch) for dusting
yellow food colouring
½ quantity Royal Icing (page 12)
a little yellow ribbon, 0.3cm/⅛in wide

● Brush the cake with Apricot Glaze and cover it with Almond Paste. Place it on the board. Reserve a small piece of Moulding Icing (Molding Frosting), about the size of an egg, and colour remainder pale yellow. Use a little to cover surface of board. Roll out remainder to a 30cm/12in square. Lay it over the cake so the icing (frosting) falls in soft folds around the sides. Smooth the icing (frosting) on top of the cake, using hands dusted with cornflour (cornstarch) and emphasize folds by stretching sections of the icing (frosting) around sides of cake with your fingers. Using a knitting needle, pierce a border of holes around edge of icing and make groups of holes on sides and top of cake for a broderie anglaise effect.

● To make the booties, reserve a quarter of the white Moulding Icing (Molding Frosting) and shape the remainder into two balls. Lengthen and flatten them slightly. Roll out the reserved icing (frosting) and cut out two 2.5cm/1in by 7.5cm/3in rectangles. Make decorative holes with knitting needle. Brush one long edge of each strip with water and secure it to the bootie bases with joins at the front. Position on top of cake.

● Colour three-quarters of the Royal Icing yellow and place it in a piping bag fitted with a plain nozzle (no. 0). Use it to pipe circles around the holes and the decorative leaves between the holes, for a broderie anglaise effect. Colour a little icing (frosting) yellow and pipe the same type of decoration on the booties. Using a plain nozzle (nos. 1 or 2) pipe decorative dots around the lower edge of the icing (frosting) and two straight lines of icing (frosting) on either side of the border holes. Use the remaining icing (frosting) to run-out the child's name on top of cake following directions on page 16. Tie a ribbon around the booties with a bow at the front.

Engagement Cake

The lace effect on this cake makes a good cover up for less than perfect flat icing! A posy of roses completes the simple design.

INGREDIENTS

25cm/10in square Rich Fruit Cake (pages 9 and 10)
1 quantity Apricot Glaze (page 11)
triple quantity Almond Paste (page 10)
30cm/12in square silver cake board
quadruple quantity Royal Icing (page 12)
cream food colouring
1.2m/4ft piece white ribbon, about 2cm/¾in wide
fresh flowers to decorate

● Make the fruit cake according to directions on pages 9 and 10.
● Brush the cake with Apricot Glaze and cover it with almond paste. Place it on the board.
● Reserve a quarter of the Royal Icing. Colour the remainder pale cream, and use it to flat ice cake and surface of board. Leave it to dry completely.
● Using a plate as a guide, mark a 23cm/9in circle on top of the cake. Using a ruler as a guide, mark 2 lines 2.5cm/1in apart around sides of cake. (The area between the lines will be left unpiped for ribbon.)
● Place some of the reserved icing (frosting) in a piping bag fitted with a medium-sized star nozzle. Use it to pipe a scroll around the top and lower edges of the cake.
● Place the remaining icing (frosting) in a piping bag fitted with a writer nozzle (no. 1) and use it to pipe a lace effect on the areas shown. This is done by holding the nozzle close to the cake and piping a continuous wiggly line. Pipe small dots over the marked circle on top of the cake and along the lines marked for ribbon. Place the ribbon around cake securing the ends with icing (frosting).
● Using same nozzle, pipe the outline of couple's name in a semi-circle on top of cake. (Get someone who's good at lettering to outline the lettering or make templates.)
● Thin down the icing (frosting) left in the bag to run-out consistency (see page 16) and colour it a darker shade of cream. Use it to run-out the lettering.
● Arrange a posy of flowers on the cake just before it is needed.

Fiftieth Anniversary Cake

This special cake can easily be adapted for a silver anniversary by using silver colouring, or a ruby anniversary using red colouring. The flower centres have been dusted with 'gold lustre', available from cake decorating specialists but cream food colouring could be used instead.

INGREDIENTS

25cm/10in square Rich Fruit Cake (pages 9 and 10)
1 quantity Apricot Glaze (page 11)
triple quantity Almond Paste (page 10)
33cm/13in square silver cake board
double quantity Moulding Icing (Molding Frosting) (page 13)
cream and gold food colourings
cornflour (cornstarch) for dusting
1.2m/4ft gold ribbon, about 0.5cm/¼in wide
½ quantity Royal Icing (page 12)
cocktail stick
gold lustre
white stamen heads

● Brush the cake with Apricot Glaze and cover with Almond Paste. Place on board.

● Colour a small piece of Moulding Icing (Molding Frosting), about the size of an apple, with cream colouring and reserve. Reserve a quarter of white Moulding Icing (Molding Frosting) and use the remainder to cover top and sides of cake.

● Reserve a little of the cream icing (frosting) for top of cake and use remainder to cover surface of board. Roll out some reserved white icing (frosting) to a 30cm/12in by 6.5cm/2½in strip. Brush the top of the underside with a little water and secure a strip to one side of the cake, allowing the lower edge to fall away from cake. Repeat on all sides of cake using remaining icing (frosting), folding icing (frosting) neatly at corners.

● Roll out reserved cream icing (frosting) to a 10cm/4in square. Secure it to the centre of cake.

● Cut the ribbon into 2cm/¾in lengths. Beginning at one corner of the cake, and using a thin-bladed knife, make a small vertical cut along the top of the strip. Press one end of the ribbon length into the cut, using a knife to ease it in. Make a second cut 2.5cm/½in along strip and push the other end of the ribbon into it. Attach the remaining ribbon to the cake in the same way. Leave it to harden.

● Using the small flower template given, mark 4 designs along the lower edge of each side of cake. Use the larger template to mark designs on top of cake.

● Place the Royal Icing in a piping bag fitted with a writer nozzle (no. 1). Use it to pipe over the outlines of the flowers on one side of the cake. Using a cocktail stick, draw a piped line into the centre of the flower to give a fluted edge. Repeat with the remaining flowers then pipe over the leaf outlines. Using more icing (frosting), pipe a small fluted border around the edge of the cake and around the cream icing on top of the cake. Use the remaining icing (frosting) to pipe lines on either side of the ribbon. (Use the same technique with the cocktail stick to give fluted finish, as for flowers).

● Colour the centres of the flowers with lustre colour and press stamen heads into centres of flowers.

● Using the template given, mark numbers on the top of the cake. Paint the numbers, leaves and piped edging with gold colouring to finish.

A Bouquet of Flowers

A Bouquet of Flowers

Combine two gifts in one with this colourful bouquet. Write the message to suit the occasion, whether it's for Mother's Day, a birthday or a retirement celebration. You could add a name-tag as in the Bowl of Daffodils Cake (page 47).

INGREDIENTS

1 quantity Quick Cake Mix (page 9)
35.5cm/14in by 25cm/10in covered board
1 quantity Apricot Glaze (page 11)
1 quantity Moulding Icing (Molding Frosting) (page 13)
cornflour (cornstarch) for dusting
red, green, pink and yellow food colourings
½ quantity Royal Icing (page 12)
30cm/12in length of ribbon, about 1cm/½in wide

● Bake the Quick Cake Mix in a 28cm/11in by 19cm/7½in shallow cake tin for about 1 hour or until surface feels firm to the touch. When completely cooled, cut one end of the cake to a point. Trim off the top edges of the cake to give it gently sloping sides. Transfer the cake to a board and brush it with apricot glaze.

● Colour a small piece of Moulding Icing (Molding Frosting), about the size of an egg, with red food colouring. Colour a second piece green, and another smaller piece pink. Reserve them for decoration.

● Reserve a piece of white icing (frosting) for decoration. Roll out the remainder into a rectangle 7.5cm/3in larger than cake. Lay it over the cake, smoothing down the sides using hands dusted with cornflour (cornstarch). Trim the edges. Roll out the trimmings into a rectangle measuring about 12.5cm/5in by 5cm/2in. Gather up one side and secure it to the pointed end of the cake.

● Colour the Royal Icing green and place half of it in a piping bag fitted with a plain nozzle (no. 3). Use it to pipe the flower stalks, starting at the pointed end of the cake and finishing where a flower will be positioned. Place the remaining Royal Icing in a piping bag fitted with a plain nozzle (no. 1) and use it to pipe small ferns at irregular intervals towards edges of cake.

● Use red Moulding Icing (Molding Frosting) to make rosebuds and fully-opened roses. Use pink and reserved white icing (frosting) to make carnations (see page 15). Secure the flowers to the tops of the stalks with icing (frosting). Roll out the green icing (frosting) and use it to make the leaves (see page 15). Arrange them amongst the flowers. Tie the ribbon in a bow and secure it around the base of the cake.

Chocolate Box

Most of us love chocolate, so this cake should suit many special occasions. If you feel like splashing out, moisten the cake with rum or an orange-flavoured liqueur before icing (frosting) it.

INGREDIENTS

1 quantity chocolate-flavoured Quick Cake Mix (page 9)
25cm/10in board, covered with shiny brown paper
1 quantity Buttercream (page 14)
2 tbsp/25g/1oz cocoa powder
225g/8oz plain (semisweet) chocolate
about 24 chocolates (chocolate candies)
chocolate sweet (candy) cases
1.5m/5ft brown or cream ribbon, about 0.5cm/¼in wide

● Bake the Quick Cake Mix in a 28cm/11in by 19cm/7½in shallow cake tin (pan) for about 1 hour. Place the cake on a board.

● Reserve a third of the buttercream and beat cocoa powder into the remainder. Use it to cover the top and sides of the cake.

● Melt the chocolate and spread it thinly on a sheet of waxed paper into a rectangle measuring about 26.5cm/10½in by 24cm/9½in. Leave it to set (see page 17). Cut out 2 23cm/9in by 6.5cm/2½in rectangles and 2 16.5cm/6½in by 6.5cm/2½in rectangles. Secure one rectangle to each side of cake. (It is worth cooling your hands under cold water first.) Cut a small message tag from chocolate trimmings and reserve it.

● Spread the reserved buttercream onto one side of the cake. Draw a serrated icing (frosting) scraper over the side, so the chocolate shows through in lines. Coat the remaining sides in the same way.

● Arrange the chocolates in the cases and place them on top of the cake.

● Place the remaining buttercream in a piping bag fitted with a writer nozzle (no. 1). Use it to pipe a message on the tag and lay it over the chocolates.

● Use a little ribbon to make a bow and secure it to the tag. Tie the remaining ribbon around the cakes, securing the ends with buttercream.

Christmas Cake

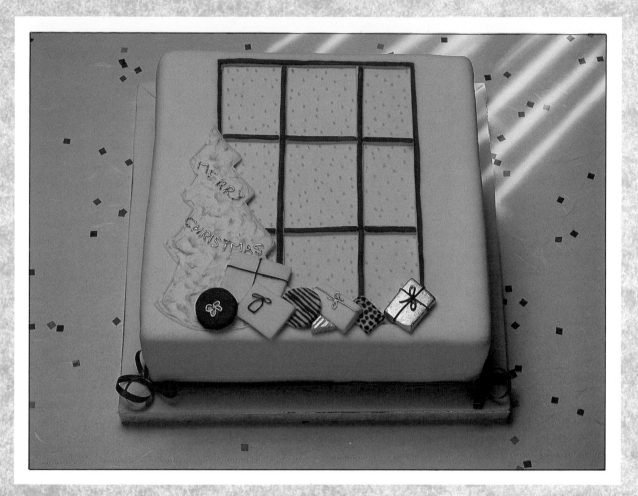

I f you want to spend a little more time on decor- ating the Christmas cake this year – try this pretty window scene.

INGREDIENTS

20cm/8in square Rich Fruit Cake (page 9)
1 quantity Apricot Glaze (page 11)
double quantity Almond Paste (page 10)
25cm/10in square silver cake board
1½ quantity Moulding Icing (Molding Frosting) (page 13)
blue, red and silver food colourings
cornflour (cornstarch) for dusting
1 cup/125g/4oz icing (confectioner's) sugar
a little egg white
about 1.5m/5ft red ribbon, 0.5cm/¼in wide

● Make the Rich Fruit Cake as on pages 9 and 10. Brush the cake with Apricot Glaze and cover with Almond Paste. Place it on a board.

● Colour a quarter of the Moulding Icing (Molding Frosting) pale blue. Roll it out on a surface dusted with cornflour (cornstarch) and use it to cover the top of the cake. Trim the edges and use them to cover the surface of the board. Dust the top of cake liberally with cornflour (cornstarch).

● Roll out the remaining icing (frosting) and use it to cover the top and sides of the cake. Trim the edges. Working fairly quickly, cut out a 19cm/7½in by 12.5cm/5in rectangle from the top of the white icing (frosting) and lift it out to expose blue icing (frosting) underneath. Roll out the trimmings and cut out half a Christmas tree. Secure it to the lower left-hand side of the 'window'. Mark the other half of the tree on the white icing (frosting) with a pin.

● To make the window panels, cut out long, thin strips of icing (frosting) about 0.3cm/⅛in wide. Dampen the undersides with water and position them as in the photograph. Use the rest to shape 'parcels'. Secure to the cake.

● Beat the icing (confectioner's) sugar with egg white until it forms stiff peaks. Spread the mixture into Christmas tree area, and roughen the surface to form peaks. Place the remaining icing (frosting) in a piping bag fitted with a writer nozzle (no. 1). Use it to pipe an outline around the Christmas tree, a 'MERRY CHRISTMAS' message and ribbon on the parcels. Use food colourings to paint the frame on the window, parcels and the writing on the tree. Tie a ribbon around the cake, securing the ends with icing (frosting).

Christmas Wreath Cake

Semi-rich, chocolatey, and above all, easy to ice, this cake is ideal for last minute bakers – or those who prefer a lighter Christmas cake.

CHRISTMAS CAKE:
⅔ cup/150g/5oz soft margarine
½ cup/150g/5oz light brown sugar
2 eggs
1¼ cups/150g/5oz self-raising (self-rising) flour
1.25ml/¼ tsp baking powder
2 tbsp/25g/1 oz cocoa powder
2.5ml/½ tsp ground cinnamon
2.5ml/½ tsp ground mixed spice
1½ cups/350g/12oz chopped mixed dried fruit
DECORATIONS:
28cm/11in round silver cake board
1 quantity Quick American Frosting (page 14)
2 leaves rice paper
1 cup/125g/4oz icing (confectioner's) sugar
green and red food colourings
1 egg white
red candles and holders

● To make the cake, grease a 1.1L/2pt ring mould (tube pan). Place the margarine, brown sugar, and eggs in a bowl. Sift together the flour, baking powder, cocoa, cinnamon and mixed spice and add this to the bowl. Beat well with an electric whisk 1 to 2 minutes until evenly blended. Stir in the dried fruit. Turn the mixture into the prepared tin (pan) and bake at 170°C/325°F/Gas 3 for about 35 to 40 minutes, or until surface feels just firm to the touch.

● Leave the cake in the tin (pan) for 10 minutes then turn it out on to a wire rack to cool.

● To decorate the cake, place the cake on the board and coat it with the American Frosting, raising it into peaks. Leave it to dry, preferably overnight.

● Cut out the holly leaves from the rice paper, using the template (see endpapers). Spoon 30ml/ 2 tbsp of the icing (confectioner's) sugar into a bowl. Add a little green food colouring and mix it until icing (confectioner's) sugar turns green but remains powdery. (This is easiest done with your hands although they may turn a little green!)

● Place remaining icing (confectioner's) sugar in a separate bowl and mix it to piping consistency with a little of the egg white. Colour the icing (frosting) red and place it in a piping bag fitted with a writer nozzle (no. 1 or no. 2). Reserve it.

● Place the green icing (confectioner's) sugar in a sieve, and sprinkle it over the surface of the cake. Press the candles and holders into the cake. Secure the holly leaves to the cake by pressing one end into the surface of the icing (frosting). Using the icing (frosting) in the piping bag pipe around the edges of the leaves to finish.

Christmas Wreath Cake

Christmas Wreath Cake

Easter Cake

Easter Cake

This pretty cake design is made with a rice paper 'cut-out' which is edible so you needn't worry about removing it before eating. A little care is needed when cutting out the design so use a good craft knife rather than scissors, work on a wooden board.

INGREDIENTS

15cm/6in square Rich Fruit Cake (pages 9 and 10)
1 quantity Apricot Glaze (page 11)
1 quantity Almond Paste (page 10)
20cm/8in square silver cake board
1 quantity Moulding Icing (Molding Frosting) (page 13)
yellow, green and violet food colourings
cornflour (cornstarch) for dusting
16.5cm/6½in square rice paper
½ quantity Royal Icing (page 12)

● Brush the cake with Apricot Glaze and cover it with Almond Paste. Place it on a board.

● Colour a small piece of Moulding Icing (Molding Frosting), about the size of an egg, with yellow food colouring. Colour a second piece pale green and a third pale violet. Divide each colour in half. Press the colours haphazardly together. Dust a surface with cornflour (cornstarch) and roll out the mixture into a square large enough to cover top of cake. (Once rolled, the colours should have blended slightly to create a marbled pastel effect.) Lay the icing (frosting) on the cake and trim the edges. Use the remaining Moulding Icing (Molding Frosting) to cover the sides of the cake and the surface of the board.

● Using the template (see endpapers), transfer the flower design on to the square of rice paper, and cut out flowers and leaves.

● Place the Royal Icing in a piping bag fitted with a basket nozzle and pipe a line around the top edge of the cake. Lay the rice paper square over the piped border, so the edges of the paper are secured to the icing (frosting). Pipe a second line of icing (frosting) over first to secure the paper. Pipe another line of icing (frosting) around the base of the cake.

● Place the remaining icing (frosting) in a piping bag fitted with a writer nozzle (no. 1). Use it to pipe an outline around the edges of the cut-out and to make the garlands around the sides of the cake.

Index

Useful Addresses

The following specialist shops have a mail order service and will supply catalogues on request. Some also have showrooms; enquire about times of opening so that you can pay them a visit.

UK

Mary Ford Cake Artistry Centre
28–30 Southbourne Grove, Southbourne,
Bournemouth, Dorset BH6 3RA
Baker Smith Ltd
65 The Street, Tongham, Farnham, Surrey
GU10 1DE
Cookcraft Club Ltd
20 Canterbury Road, Herne Bay, Kent CT6 5DJ
Homebakers Supplies
157–159 High Street, Wolstanton, Newcastle, Staffs
ST5 0EJ (Tel 0782 614119)
Guy Paul and Co Ltd
Unit B4, A1 Industrial Park, Little End Road, Eaton
Socon, Cambs PE19 3JH
Covent Garden Kitchen Supplies
3 North Row, The Market, Covent Garden,
London WC2
David Mellor
4 Sloane Square, London SW1W 8EE

USA

Wilton Enterprises Inc
2240 West 75th Street, Woodridge, Illinois 60517
H. Roth & Son Paprika Co
1577 First Avenue, New York NY 10028
Paprikas Weiss
1546 2nd Avenue, New York NY 10021
Bridge Co
214 East 52nd Street, New York NY 10022
The Country Store
2255 CR 27, Waterloo, Indiana 46793
Parrish's Cake Decorating Supplies
314 West 58th Street, Los Angeles, California 90037
All About Cakes
11510 Woodside Avenue, Santee, California 92071

Acknowledgements

The author would like to thank Mary Ford Cake Artistry Centre Ltd for kindly supplying some of the items for photography.

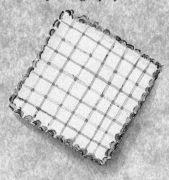

123456

MAKING A WISH